HEATHROW AIRPORT
THE FIRST 25 YEARS

HEATHROW AIRPORT
THE FIRST 25 YEARS

CHARLES WOODLEY

The
History
Press

Starting young. The author and his mother in the north side spectators' enclosure in the early 1950s. (Author)

First published 2010
Reprinted 2012

The History Press
The Mill, Brimscombe Port
Stroud, Gloucestershire, GL5 2QG
www.thehistorypress.co.uk

British Library Cataloguing in Publication Data.
A catalogue record for this book is available from the British Library.

ISBN 978 0 7524 5300 2

Typesetting and origination by The History Press
Printed and bound in Great Britain by
Marston Book Services Limited, Didcot

CONTENTS

INTRODUCTION

Today, Heathrow is a major transportation crossroads, with thousands of flights each year conveying millions of passengers to all parts of the globe. But its position as London's premier airport only came about as the result of an act of subterfuge which saw prime agricultural land being requisitioned under wartime emergency powers, ostensibly for a base for long-range RAF transport aircraft. Once the true purpose became known, the airport was constructed and brought into service in haste; passengers had to put up with leaky marquees as terminal facilities until temporary pre-fabricated buildings could be erected.

Despite the primitive conditions at first, the airport flourished and grew to such an extent that the original buildings on the north side were outgrown within a few years and the design and construction of a new terminal complex and control tower commenced. This was to be in the centre of the pattern of runways and linked to the outside world by a tunnel beneath one of them. When the complex opened in 1955, Britain at last had a world-class airport to be proud of, one which attracted large numbers of sightseers every weekend. This had in fact been the case since the airport opened in 1946, and the authorities had always been keen to attract potential passengers by providing enclosures from which they could watch the action close up. It was not just the scheduled airline comings and goings that attracted spectators. In its early years the airport was the starting point for an air race to New Zealand and many speed and altitude record attempts, the venue for static displays of the RAF's latest fighters and bombers on Battle of Britain Days, and had even staged a garden party in the centre of the airfield while the airliners came and went. Visitors to the spectators' enclosures could not only watch the flying, they could go aloft themselves on sightseeing flights over central London.

The new Central Area buildings continued the theme of public access, with extensive roof gardens, complete with coin-operated telescopes and coach tours of the airport. However, in 1969 Terminal One opened, and as well as being the first terminal at Heathrow to be reserved for the use of just one airline and the companies it handled, it was also the first not to incorporate any public viewing facilities. Later, a visitor centre was opened on the original north side of the airport, but this was to be short-lived and from then on the public were discouraged from sightseeing at the airport they had financed with their taxes in its early years. It is at around this time that my account of what I consider the airport's 'vintage years' concludes. I hope this volume will bring back fond memories for those of mellow years and provide younger readers with a glimpse into happier, more innocent days at Heathrow.

ACKNOWLEDGEMENTS

Keith Hayward and all the helpers at the British Airways Archives and Museum for supplying copies of correspondence and magazine articles.

Air-Britain (Historians) Ltd for permission to reproduce images from their black and white photo library.

All the contributors to the Air-Britain Information Exchange website for answering my queries and supplying additional material.

And all the following for supplying photographs, images and encouragement: Heathrow Airport plc press office; Frank Hudson, Mick West, Michael Wall, P.J.S. Pearson, David Bowler, Steve Bond, Vic Attwood, Eric Loseby, John Carter, John Hamlin, The Ricky Shiels Collection, Maurice Marsh, Malcolm D. Stride, Michael H. Starritt, Peter Maddocks and the press offices of British Aerospace plc, Lufthansa, Air France and SABENA.

If there is anyone I have forgotten, please accept my apologies and thanks.

1

THE ORIGINS OF HEATHROW

There are at least two theories regarding the origin of the place name Heathrow. One suggests that it was named after a man called John Heath, on whose estate the land now occupied by the airport once stood. John Heath was a 'Judge of Common Please' (pleas), and the cousin of Dr Benjamin Heath, the famous Harrow School headmaster. John Heath ended his days on his estate. Another theory suggests that the name derives from a hamlet called 'Heath Row' which was demolished during the construction of the airport (it stood on the site of today's Terminal Three). The name Heath Row can be found on maps and documents dating back several hundred years to long before Judge Heath was born. It was the smallest of the four villages and hamlets (the others being Longford, Sipson and Harmondsworth) which made up the parish of Harmondsworth. The name was first mentioned in 1453, and in old records – including the Harmondsworth Parish Registers of 1860 – it is usually written as one word. It appears on John Rocque's 1754 map of Middlesex as Heath Row, and was included (but spelt 'Hetherow') on Ogilvy's map of Middlesex of 1675.

In 1930, Charles Richard Fairey, a forty-six-year-old aero engineer and aircraft builder, paid the vicar of Harmondsworth £15,000 for a 150-acre plot of land on which he intended to build a private airfield for the assembly and testing of aircraft. Over the next ten years the site was to bear various names, including Great West Aerodrome, Harmondsworth Aerodrome, and Heath Row Aerodrome. The airfield was located between the Bath Road to the north, and the Great South West road to the south-east. In the north-east corner was erected the biggest aircraft hangar of its kind at the time. The first aircraft to use the aerodrome was a Fairey Hendon bomber which was delivered in sections, assembled, and test flown on 25 November 1930.

Since the First World War, several other sites in the vicinity had been used as airfields. Part of Hounslow Heath was used as an airfield by the Royal Flying Corps during that conflict, and at the end of the war it became Hounslow Heath Aerodrome, opening as London's first airport on 1 April 1919. Soon afterwards, regular flights to Paris commenced, and the first ever flight from England to Australia took off from Hounslow Heath on 12 November 1919. The airport was closed down in 1920 and its services transferred to Croydon. From 1917, Hanworth Park was used by Whitehead Aircraft Ltd of Feltham for test flights and delivery flights. Flying there ceased at the end of the First World War, and did not resume until 1928, when 229 acres were laid out as London Airpark by National Flying Services Ltd, with Hanworth House serving as the clubhouse. During the Second World War, it was used by the General Aircraft Co. for their Hamilcar gliders and other aircraft. In 1946 flying ceased because of its proximity to Heathrow, and in 1959 it became a public park. Heston Aerodrome started life in 1928 when Airwork Ltd bought 170 acres of land between the rural villages of Heston and Cranworth. The official opening was on 6 July 1929, but by 1934 Airwork was losing money on the airfield and decided to sell it. In November 1936, the Air Ministry reluctantly decided to buy the airfield and much of the surrounding land to develop into an airport to replace Croydon. It was used by Prime Minister Neville Chamberlain in 1938 as the departure point for his visits to Hitler in Munich. Plans for extensive expansion would have made Heston the largest civil aerodrome in Britain, but these were frustrated by the outbreak of the Second World War. Heston Airport closed in 1947.

In 1943, Professor Patrick Abercrombie, a distinguished town planner and Vice President of the Royal Institute of British Architects, was put in charge of the creation of the Greater London Plan, which was published in 1944. His brief included air transport requirements, and fifty-two possible sites for airports around London were considered. The Plan predicted a need for up to ten different airports to serve London for various purposes. Among the sites favoured for development were Heston, Bovingdon, Hatfield, Matching (Essex), Fairlop (north-east London), Lullingstone (Kent), West Malling, Gatwick and Croydon. Top of the list was an area twelve miles west of Victoria Station called Heathrow. It stood on level land with a gravel subsoil and measured three and a half miles by three miles. Plans for its possible expansion envisaged the procurement of further land to the north of the Bath Road.

2

THE DECEPTION OVER HEATHROW

In 1944 Harold Balfour, a former Royal Flying Corps pilot, was Under Secretary of State for Air, working closely with Lord Beaverbrook, Prime Minister Winston Churchill's Arms Minister. Throughout the course of the war, he had often pondered on the future shape of British civil aviation post-war. He was aware that there would be a huge demand for air transport to and from London, and had been keeping a close eye on Richard Fairey's Great West Aerodrome. While Professor Abercrombie was working on his report, Harold Balfour was working behind the scenes to cut through the 'red tape' and have a suitable site for a major civil airport for London ready for development as soon as the war ended. He was aware that the Great West Aerodrome was the ideal site for London's main airport. He was also aware that any attempt to acquire the land for this purpose would involve long and complicated civil procedures, including a public enquiry, and would provoke objections from other ministries such as Agriculture and Housing. As the defeat of Germany was only a matter of time away, the Government was heavily involved in planning for the subsequent conquest of the Japanese mainland. To accomplish this would require airfields with runways of extended length for the speedy transportation of troops and supplies to the Far East. A powerful document was put together for the Cabinet, stating that the requisitioning of the Great West Aerodrome and a large area of land around under wartime emergency powers would provide the basis for the creation of an RAF transport base, which could supply Britain's long-range military transportation needs. In fact, several existing bomber airfields in the Home Counties could have served the purpose just as well, and the site was never really intended for military use, but Winston Churchill formed a committee to take the matter further. This committee included Lord Beaverbrook, who Harold Balfour took into his confidence as to the real purpose of the acquisition. As expected, objections were received from the Ministry for Agriculture and the Ministry for Housing, but the Cabinet came down on Balfour's side and the necessary land was requisitioned under the Defence of the Realm Act 1939, which did not permit any appeal.

On 31 May 1944, a compulsory purchase order was drawn up to cover some 2,800 acres including the hamlets of Heath Row and Perry Oaks and the Great West Aerodrome. Richard Fairey was told he would have to vacate the airfield to make way for a new RAF Transport Command base to support the Tiger Force in the war against Japan. Fairey flight testing was transferred to Heston and White Waltham, and work on the redevelopment commenced in June 1944. Emphasis was laid on completing the runways before any buildings. Fairey Aviation finally moved out in July 1945, although the Fairey hangar was to survive to become the oldest building on the airport, being used by the airport fire service until at least August 1952.

The sudden ending of the war against Japan ended any pretence of plans for military use of the site and left the way clear for civil development. On 23 May 1945, the Labour Party won a General Election and Churchill, Beaverbrook and Balfour were evicted from office. The new Aviation Minister, Lord Winster, announced that the new airport for London was top of his Government's agenda and that operations from it would commence while construction work was still taking place. He did not mention that the project was likely to cost £25 million, the largest sum ever allocated to a single Government-funded project. The press demanded to know its location, but the Air Ministry kept this a secret until 31 May, when the plans were disclosed to Middlesex County Council. Even then the exact location was kept under a press blackout for some time afterwards.

3

CONSTRUCTION BEGINS

Work on the new airport commenced with the emphasis on the runways, and the main east-west runway was ready by September 1945. In December of that year, British South American Airways selected the airport as the departure point for a series of experimental flights to South America, prior to the establishment of scheduled services. The fledgling airline also picked out several RAF buildings for its use during the proving flights and afterwards. Building 13 would be used as offices for the station manager and his traffic staff; building 64 would be used as a radio and radar workshop; building 41 would house maintenance personnel, and building 1 would be used by HM Customs as a freight shed.

BSAA was made aware that no flying control or signals facilities would be provided and that they would have to make their own arrangements for these. The airline inspected the former Fairey hangar and considered it suitable for aircraft maintenance, but it was hampered by its lack of direct access to the runway. The RAF agreed to make a crash tender available but said that BSAA would have to make its own manning arrangements pending the eventual appointment of crews by the Ministry of Civil Aviation. BSAA had already made its own arrangements for the supply of fuel. The departure date of the first proving flight to South America was set for 1 January 1946, and on this date the airport site was formerly transferred from the Air Ministry to the Ministry of Civil Aviation. Due ceremony was observed, and the following itinerary was arranged with military precision for the official party led by Lord Winster, the Minister of Aviation:

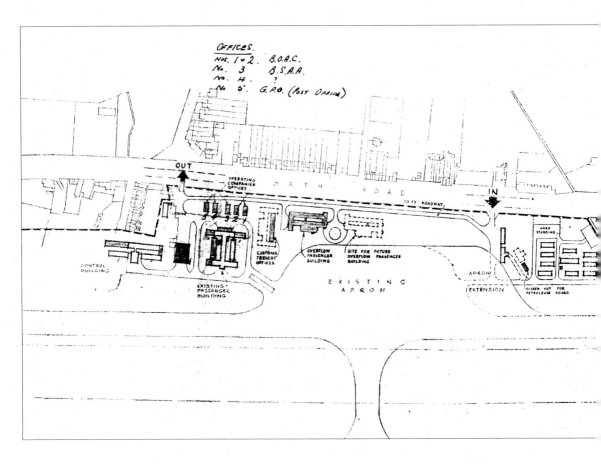

10.45 a.m.	Party arrives by motor coach from London, assembling at the control tower.
10.45–11.00	Inspection of main runway from top of control tower.
11.00	Party re-assembles in motor coaches for tour of site.
11.05	Coaches pass RAF camp, going towards eastern end of main runway.
11.05–11.15	Inspection of FIDO (Fog, Intensive Dispersal Of). Crossing of intersection of runway 3.
11.15–11.20	Coaches travel down runway 3.
11.20–11.25	Inspection of runway 3 concrete mixing plant.
11.25–11.30	Coaches proceed down runway 3.
11.30–11.35	Inspection of concrete spreading plant at work on runway 3.

A plan of the airport buildings and apron areas on the north side in April 1946. (Via Keith Hayward, British Airways Archives)

11.35–11.40	Coaches proceed along Heathrow Road to Pond C.
11.40–11.45	Inspection of Pond C area.
11.45–11.55	Coaches return to control tower.
12.00	AVM Bennett takes off on initial flight to South America.
12.25	Re-assemble in coaches.
12.25–12.30	Coaches proceed to Main Workmen's Camp.
12.30–1.30	Buffet lunch in Recreation Hall at Main Workmen's Camp.
1.30	Re-assemble in coaches and return to control tower for flights (local circuit of airfield in BOAC Dakota).

The proving flight to South America was commanded by AVM D.C. Bennett, and the First Officer was Wing Commander R.C. Alabaster. Also aboard the BSAA Avro

Lancastrian G-AGWG *Star Light* was BSAA 'Star Girl' Mary Guthrie, a former Air Transport Auxiliary pilot and now Britain's first post-war air hostess. In his speech at the ceremony Lord Winster said:

On this first day of the New Year this proving flight starts off from Heathrow, which will be the future civil airport of London, and it takes off from the finest runway in the world. I think it's a happy omen for the flight that yesterday's fog has cleared away, and Air Vice Marshall Bennett, who leads the flight, will take off in fine, bright, clear weather. To me this aeroplane, with its beautiful name *Star Light*, is a symbol of the determination of our country to regain our place in the markets of the world and to use the air as a means of cultivating good relations with other nations, and cultivating with them the arts of peace. Air Vice Marshall Bennett pioneered the transatlantic delivery of aircraft during the war. Today he starts off on another pioneering job, and this flight is the first step towards the establishment of a swift and regular British air service to South America. Air Vice Marshall Bennett and all who fly with him today are truly representing the spirit and determination of this country to play the same leading part in the air that it has always played at sea. I wish them all Godspeed and a pleasant and successful journey.

In his reply AVM Bennett said:

We are about to take off on our first flight and about to do so with a fast four-engined airliner of proven quality. It has those things which are necessary for an airline; safety, speed and comfort. Our airline will start within a few weeks, immediately following this proving flight. We hope to offer the peoples of this country and of South America services of which they will be proud and they will be happy to use. On this, the first day of 1946, we propose to take the first practical steps in getting that going.

On board the Lancastrian that day were a total of eight crew and ten passengers, each of whom had paid £190 2s 0d for a one-way ticket to Montevideo or £192 6s 0d for a passage to Buenos Aires. The flight routed via Lisbon, Bathurst, Natal, Rio de Janeiro and Montevideo. Once the aircraft had taken off the airport was closed down again until the Lancastrian returned eighteen days later.

During 1946, a Cabinet Committee on Civil Aviation was set up. This envisaged the development of Heathrow in three stages.

Stage 1 was to be completed by 31 December 1947 and entailed the compulsory purchase of all the land required south of the Bath Road. This meant the acquisition of 2,650 acres of land, including the 1,590 acres already requisitioned by the RAF under the Defence of The Realm Act, and the demolition of 215 houses.

Stage 2 was to be completed by 31 December 1949 but did not require the acquisition of further land or buildings.

Stage 3 was to be completed during the period 1950-1953 and involved the extension of the airport north of the Bath Road. No specific dates were given for this but it was likely to require the purchase of a further 1,600 acres of land and the re-housing of the occupants of 950 houses.

A contemporary article in the *Middlesex Chronicle* newspaper titled 'Heathrow will show the world', quoted unofficial estimates of the cost of the airport to date as being in the region of £20 million. The 1,500 acres or so of land already acquired included about 120 acres of ponds and disused gravel workings, parts of which were traversed by the main runway. Some 200 lorries, forty mechanical excavators and fifty bulldozers were in use, and over 1,000 men were housed on the site in workmens' camps.

At the end of January 1946, the accommodation requirements for the nationalised airlines BOAC and BSAA were assessed as follows: for BOAC European services, immediate accommodation for 100 aircrew and 150 engineering personnel. For BSAA, ten huts, two for the accommodation of personnel and eights for offices and stores. It was agreed to allot to BSAA Hut Nos 41-48, 64 and 71, and the use of the latrines and ablutions in Huts 39 and 40. Hut No.27 was to be altered to serve as a passenger handling building and as overflow accommodation for BOAC personnel on European services. Hut No.25 was to be used to provide messing facilities for these staff as well as BSAA employees, and BOAC were to get all the remaining huts.

In February 1946, Sir John D'Albiac was appointed Commandant of the airport. On 15 March, following successful proving flights, BSAA began the first regular British air services to South America. Avro Lancastrians served Buenos Aires via stops at Lisbon, Bathurst, Natal, Rio de Janeiro and Montevideo. By 25 March 1946, work had been completed on the 38ft-high control tower, at that time the only brick-built structure on the airport, and a series of prefabricated huts had been assembled alongside to house the meteorological officers, teleprinter and radio staff. A special demonstration of modern transport aircraft at the airport was attended by Lord Winster and Members of Parliament from both Houses. The line-up of aircraft comprised: BSAA Lancastrian G-AGWI *Star Land*. RAF Avro York MW128.; Avro Tudor 1 prototype G-AGRC; Bristol 170 proto-type G-AGPV; RAF Handley Page Halifax C.VIII PP280; BOAC Dakota G-AGNC; Auster J/1 G-AGTY; Avro 19 G-AGPG; BOAC Avro York G-AGNX; Miles Aerovan 2 G-AGWO; Miles M.28 G-AGVX; Miles M.48 G-AGOY; Percival Proctor V G-AGTC; Vickers Viking G-AGOM.

The aircraft were open for internal inspection and the BOAC Dakota and RAF York carried the VIPs on demonstration flights. During the occasion Lord Winster announced that Heathrow would henceforth be known as 'The London Airport'. One of the reasons given for this change was that Heathrow was difficult for many foreigners to pronounce.

By April 1946, the intention was to develop the area south of the Bath Road as rapidly as possible, so as to provide six runways in total. One of these, 9,000ft long, was already in use. Two subsidiary runways, each 6,000ft long, were in an advanced stage of construction and due to be ready in July. The runways were numbered as follows: Runway No.1 was the east-west runway on the northern side of the airport. Parallel to this on the south side was unway No.5. Running north-east-south-west were Runway No.2 on the east side and Runway No.7 on the west side. Running south-east-north-west were runway Nos 6, 3 and 4. Although these designations were still in use on diagrams of the airport until as late as the early 1960s, they were probably only used for civil engineering purposes. Air traffic controllers and pilots almost certainly used the abbreviated compass headings (runway 28R/10L etc.), as reference to runway no.1, for instance, would give no indication of the landing direction.

Development of the area to the north of the Bath Road was not due to start for at least another five years. When it did, the Bath Road would have to be diverted to the north of the new airport boundary. The work was to be phased, to comply with the need to minimise demolitions while the current housing shortage continued, and to maximise the amount of agricultural land under cultivation during the next few years. The airfield at Heston was now considered to be out of date and would in any case have to close because of its proximity to London Airport. The land made available by this closure would do much to compensate for the loss of building and agricultural land swallowed up by the expansion of the new airport. The buildings at Heston could be utilised by the British airlines as stores, motor transport depots etc.

In its editorial for 29 March 1946, the aeronautical magazine *Flight* was speculating as to the eventual layout of London Airport:

Furthermore, if one examines the layout of the airfield carefully, it becomes clear that the permanent terminal buildings were to be built outside the main perimeter of the airfield- NOT alongside the Bath Road but on some other obvious vacant space, such as that in the south-east corner of the airfield. No one planning an airfield of this nature would be likely to put temporary terminal facilities on the site which was required for the permanent buildings. Then again, a control tower intended to be other than temporary is not likely to be built facing south, so that the controllers have to stare into the sun all day…What is happening then about the final plans for Heathrow? It is reasonable to suppose that the MCA does not want to commit itself publicly until at least a substantial part of the future plans for the airfield are cut and dried, but it is already well known that there is a proposal to take over a large area of land to the north of the Bath Road and to extend the airfield in this direction.

South America featured prominently in the early operations from the airport. On 16 April 1946, Lockheed L-049 Constellation PP-PCF of Panair do Brasil landed on a proving flight from Rio de Janeiro, and became the first Constellation, and the first aircraft of a foreign airline, to land at London Airport. On 22 April, BSAA Lancastrian G-AGWI *Star Land* under the command of AVM Bennett departed on another route survey flight, this time on the routeing London-Buenos Aires-Santiago de Chile-Lima-Bogota-Caracas-Trinidad-Natal-Bathurst-London, arriving back on 5 May. While it was away, Panair do Brasil commenced weekly scheduled services to London from Rio via Recife, Dakar, Lisbon and Paris.

On 1 May the Ministry of Civil Aviation took over responsibility for the allocation of permanent aircraft parking spaces on the apron from BOAC. At a BOAC meeting held at the airport on 13 May to ascertain the minimum facilities required/available at London Airport, the following information came to light; out of the fourteen huts on the site BOAC were using six of them as dormitories. BSAA held the remaining eight, using them as offices and stores. BOAC also occupied the officers and sergeants messes, also using them as dormitory accommodation. Of the total of 261 beds available, 233 were allocated to BOAC staff engaged on European operations. The staff canteen was run by BEA, but it was recommended that it be handed over to another operator. Facilities were considered to meet all current requirements. In the passenger terminal only a buffet service was provided. To meet the needs of in-flight catering, space and facilities were needed to provide meals for 224 passengers and 160 crew members each week. BOAC considered that it would need to take over four of the eight huts held by BSAA, plus the former NAAFI building currently used as a club, and a shed on the tarmac currently being used to store BSAA equipment.

At this particular time in the airport's development the passenger accommodation comprised ex-military brown marquees, which doubled as waiting rooms and arrival and departure terminals for the rest of 1946. The floors were uneven and consisted of a mixture of clinker and sand covered with coconut matting. The main marquee had windows which overlooked the apron. It was furnished with comfortable chintz arm-chairs and settees and small tables with vases of fresh flowers. Passengers could buy tea and coffee from a small refreshment stall at one end, and there were facilities for sending Western Union telegrams. Next to the exit flap was a blackboard with take-off times chalked on it. Airline staff would call the passengers to assemble them before escorting them across duckboards to the tarmac and their aircraft. The marquees also contained the newest branch of W.H.Smith & Son. This had been transferred from Strawberry Hill station in Twickenham, and sold cigarettes and tobacco in addition to newspapers and magazines. Between July and December 1946 it generated the encouraging amount of £2,000 in sales. During the same period the following year sales would exceed £6,000, making it the company's most profitable (and smallest!) outlet. Toilet facilities at the airport were of the Elsan chemical variety, although there was one flushing toilet, tucked away between two marquees. When the weather was hot the canvas walls of the marquees could be removed to allow a breeze to blow through. However, the summer of 1946 was very wet. There was no heating, and when it rained buckets and bowls had to be brought in to cope with the leaks in the marquees. Outside, duckboards formed a path through the mud. A row of red telephone boxes and a mobile post office stood outside the marquees, and dozens of RAF mobile caravans and trailers were in use by airlines, customs and immigration officers and retail staff. The original control tower was a three-storey brick building with a metal glazed visual control room located on the roof. Single-storey blocks extended to the east and west, the east block housing the meteorological office and the crew briefing section. The ground floor and the first floor of the control tower were primarily occupied by telecommunications staff and their equipment, although female air traffic control staff were able to use one of the ground -floor rooms for sleeping during the night. On the second floor was the approach control room, and on the roof behind the visual control room was accommodation for the occupants of the rudimentary spectators' enclosure. This facility proved very popular with the public. The entrance fee was 3d per person, with car parking at 1s. In its first three weeks of operation the enclosure took over £600, which was put towards the airport's operating costs.

On 28 May 1946 the joint BOAC/QANTAS 'Kangaroo' service to Australia began using London Airport on an irregular basis. The first departure was operated by BOAC Lancastrian G-AGLS, and was BOAC's first long-haul scheduled service from London Airport. At that time, BOAC's No.2 Line, which operated Lancastrians and Yorks, was still based at Hurn, near Bournemouth. On the day before a scheduled service, a crew car would pick up the duty crew from the Bournemouth area and take them to London Airport, where they would spend the night. In the meantime, their aircraft would be ferried across for them. The service operated as flight 7Q on the outward journey to Sydney and as flight 8Q on the way back. BOAC crews took the Lancastrian as far as Karachi, where a QANTAS crew took over. The first leg of the journey was a twelve-hour flight to Lydda in Palestine, where a fresh BOAC crew took over for the eight-hour leg to Karachi. Despite the lack of cooking or reheating facilities on board, the crew still managed to serve a four-course hot meal, the food being carried aboard in RAF-issue two-gallon flasks. BOAC also operated Avro Yorks, on routes to Calcutta and to Cairo, and on the long haul to Johannesburg in a special twelve-passenger layout. In early June 1946 the Lancastrians, Yorks, and many of BOAC's Dakotas were transferred from Hurn, with the rest of the Hurn activities scheduled for transfer by 15 June.

4

OPEN FOR BUSINESS

On 31 May 1946 London Airport was formally opened by Lord Winster. The Cabinet Committee on Civil Aviation had earlier rejected a proposal that the airport be named 'St George's Airport'. In his speech Lord Winster said:

> Because the airport will be the first piece of England on which thousands of foreign visitors will land I attach great importance to the design of the terminal buildings, which will be among the finest of their kind in the country. The layout of the airport will also be improved so as to be capable of handling 160 aircraft movements an hour in good weather and 120 in bad.

He also told the press that he envisaged the airport eventually having six runways, comprising three parallel pairs arranged around a central terminal building accessed by a tunnel extending from near a Staines Road entrance to near the Bath Road entrance. Plans published three weeks later caused alarm, as they showed the airport extending north of the Bath Road towards Harlington and West Drayton and also south-east to the site of today's Terminal Four. The villages of Poyle and Sipson would be engulfed, up to 1,200 houses would need to be demolished, and over 11,000 people displaced. The Ministry of Civil Aviation predicted that 1,450 staff would work for them at the airport by the end of 1946, rising to 8,000 in 1950 and 10,000 by 1954. The total number of people working at the airport for all employers was expected to total almost 10,000 over the course of the coming few years, and there was talk of a new satellite town being built to house the airport workers.

On 31 May 1946, the airport was made available for use by US airlines, on the understanding that no office accommodation could be provided for them, and that the US authorities must hold themselves responsible for any criticism about inefficient handling

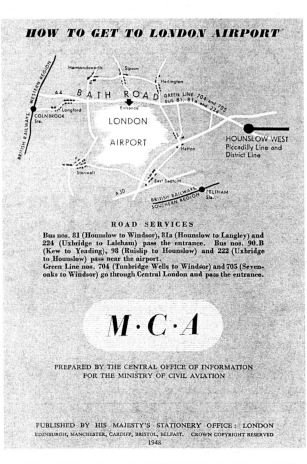

HOW TO GET TO LONDON AIRPORT

ROAD SERVICES

Bus nos. 81 (Hounslow to Windsor), 81a (Hounslow to Langley) and 224 (Uxbridge to Laleham) pass the entrance. Bus nos. 90.B (Kew to Yeading), 98 (Ruislip to Hounslow) and 222 (Uxbridge to Hounslow) pass near the airport.
Green Line nos. 704 (Tunbridge Wells to Windsor) and 705 (Sevenoaks to Windsor) go through Central London and pass the entrance.

M·C·A

PREPARED BY THE CENTRAL OFFICE OF INFORMATION
FOR THE MINISTRY OF CIVIL AVIATION

PUBLISHED BY HIS MAJESTY'S STATIONERY OFFICE: LONDON
EDINBURGH, MANCHESTER, CARDIFF, BRISTOL, BELFAST. CROWN COPYRIGHT RESERVED
1948

Left: Extract from a 1948 MCA guidebook to London Airport, giving details of public transport routes. (Via Author)

Opposite: Plans of the interior layout of the temporary north side terminal buildings in late 1946, with ideas for possible improvements to the immigration section. (Via Keith Hayward, British Airways Archives)

Below: Diagram from a 1956 publication showing the runway layout and the old-style runway numbering, as well as the notation based on compass headings. (Via Author)

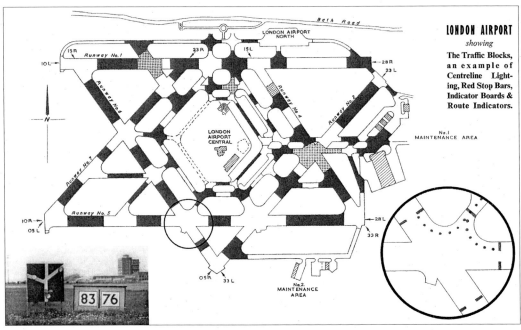

LONDON AIRPORT
showing
The Traffic Blocks, an example of Centreline Lighting, Red Stop Bars, Indicator Boards & Route Indicators.

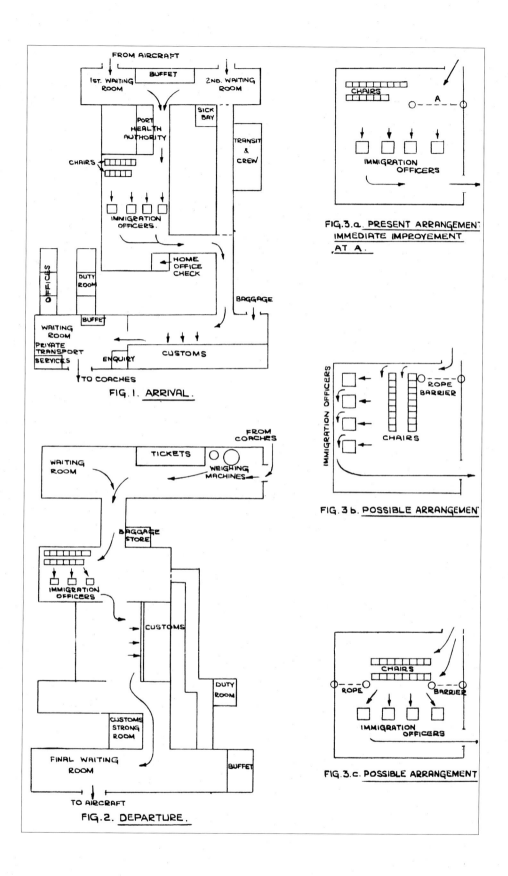

FROM AIRCRAFT

| 1ST. WAITING ROOM | BUFFET | 2ND. WAITING ROOM |

PORT HEALTH AUTHORITY

SICK BAY

TRANSIT & CREW

CHAIRS

IMMIGRATION OFFICERS.

HOME OFFICE CHECK

OFFICES

DUTY ROOM

BUFFET

BAGGAGE

WAITING ROOM

PRIVATE TRANSPORT SERVICES

ENQUIRY

CUSTOMS

TO COACHES

FIG.1. ARRIVAL.

FROM COACHES

WAITING ROOM

TICKETS

WEIGHING MACHINES

BAGGAGE STORE

IMMIGRATION OFFICERS

CUSTOMS

DUTY ROOM

CUSTOMS STRONG ROOM

FINAL WAITING ROOM

BUFFET

TO AIRCRAFT

FIG.2. DEPARTURE.

CHAIRS

A

IMMIGRATION OFFICERS

FIG.3.a. PRESENT ARRANGEMENT IMMEDIATE IMPROVEMENT AT A.

IMMIGRATION OFFICERS

ROPE BARRIER

CHAIRS

FIG.3 b. POSSIBLE ARRANGEMENT

CHAIRS

ROPE

BARRIER

IMMIGRATION OFFICERS

FIG.3.c. POSSIBLE ARRANGEMENT

that might arise as a result of the current inadequacy of the airport facilities. In preparation for the official opening of the airport, the following items were to be made available for initial operations: fourteen tents (twelve for passenger handling and two for hire to US airlines for storage), two lean-to tents for use as Elsan-equipped toilets, twenty caravans for use by customs and immigration authorities, including ten to be hired to US airlines, coconut matting for floor covering in tents, folding camp beds for use in caravans, oil heaters for passenger-handling tents. The provision of electric lighting was also to be looked into, NAAFI buildings to be used initially as staff restaurant and for aircraft catering.

The day of the opening of scheduled operations was one of high winds, driving rain and hail. The first arrivals from the USA were pipped to the post by a BOAC Lancastrian on the joint BOAC/QANTAS service from Australia. This service normally operated into Hurn but special arrangements had been made for it to use London Airport that day. It arrived two hours ahead of schedule with the help of strong tailwinds. It was followed by a Pan American 'Clipper' flight operated by Lockheed Constellation NC88860 *Clipper London*, and an American Overseas Airlines 'Flagship' Constellation, believed to be NC90923 *Flagship of Great Britain*. Both arrived from New York's La Guardia Airport within a few minutes of each other. The Pan American Constellation landed first, but it was arranged that both aircraft would shut down their engines and disembark their passengers simultaneously. Waiting to greet the passengers was a delegation of parliamentarians and air attaches from many countries, plus Lord Winster. A short while later a scheduled American Overseas Airlines DC-4 service also landed. Among the AOA passengers was General Harold R. Harris, the airline's Vice-President and General Manager, who made the point that the temporary use of marquees for the terminal buildings was more than compensated for by the elimination of the tedious three-hour road journey from Hurn into London.

Avro Lancastrian G-AGWK of British South American Airways, one of the first operators at the airport, in 1946. (Frank Hudson via airliners.net)

Silver City Airways Avro Lancastrian G-AHBT *City of New York* in 1947. (Frank Hudson via airliners.net)

At the beginning of June 1946, BOAC extended its five-times weekly Montreal-Prestwick Liberator service onwards to London, and on 4 June the 'Springbok' service to South Africa began using London Airport on a full-time basis. The fact that London Airport and nearby Northolt were within each other's airfield circuits led to the institution of special circuit rules designed to avoid collisions. When the landing direction at Northolt was easterly or south-easterly a left-handed circuit was made, with a right-handed circuit being used when landings were in the opposite direction. At London Airport a right-handed circuit was made when landings on the single were made towards the east. In the event of bad weather BOAC's designated diversion airfields were (in order of preference) Blackbushe, Northolt, Hurn and RAF Valley in North Wales. On 11 June, BSAA Avro York G-AHEW *Star Leader* became the first aircraft to land at London Airport after a non-stop flight from North America, when it flew direct from Gander on the last leg of a week-long Shell Oil charter to Caracas and back. Five days later the first of BOAC's new Lockheed Constellations arrived on a non-stop proving flight from New York. The improved productivity of the Constellations was to lead to a reduction of $50 on the New York-London single fare, from $375 to $325. By July BOAC's services from London Airport included the following; a three-times weekly 'Springbok' Avro York service to South Africa, three Lancastrian services each week to Sydney, a similar number of Avro York services to Cairo and Calcutta, a twice-weekly service to Cairo, Dakota services daily to Cairo, three-times weekly to West Africa, and once-weekly to Lydda.

Trans–Canada Air Lines Avro Lancaster CF-CMX with a Constellation taking off in the background on 30 May 1948. (Frank Hudson via airliners.net)

Avro Lancastrian G-AGMG and an Air France Dakota amidst the building works on the north side in 1947. (Frank Hudson via airliners.net)

Skyways Avro York G-AHFI and a Constellation on 10 November 1946. Note the building work in progress and the lack of barriers. (Frank Hudson via airliners.net)

BOAC Dakota G-AGKG and two compatriots at the airport in its early days. (Via Author)

BOAC Avro York G-AGNS taxies into the north side area. (Air-Britain)

Part of the tented terminal facilities in 1946, complete with telephone boxes and letterbox. (Heathrow Airport plc)

Passengers walk across a wet and blustery tarmac to their Avro Lancastrian for the inaugural BOAC scheduled service from the new London Airport on 28 May 1946. (Heathrow Airport plc)

BOAC's major servicing was still carried out at Hurn and Bovingdon, but flight checks were done at London Airport. Mr G.R. Hawtin, BOAC's Station Manager, had a staff of around 300, and a fleet of BOAC coaches linked the airport with Airways Terminal at Victoria, London. In July 1946, several car hire companies were offered non-exclusive rights at London Airport and Northolt by the Ministry of Aviation. Their operations were to be on an experimental basis, as at that time there was no proper office accommodation or surfaced car parks for them to use at the airport. The initial contract was to be for three months, after which the Ministry hoped to be able to put the contract out to tender.

BOAC Dakota G-AGHF and another example at the airport in its infancy. (Via Author)

BOAC Avro Lancastrian G-AKPZ. (Via Author)

BOAC Lancastrian G–AGLS takes off on the first BOAC scheduled service from London Airport on 28 May 1946. In the background building work goes on. (Via Author)

BOAC Avro Lancastrian G–AGMG *Nicosia* runs up. (The Ricky Shiels Collection)

The interior of one of the marquees used as the passenger terminal in 1946. Next to the W.H. Smith stall is a blackboard giving flight information. (Heathrow Airport plc)

Passengers huddle from the rain under Pan American Constellation NC88860 on 31 May 1946 after arriving from New York on the first transatlantic scheduled service into London Airport. Behind the period cars can be seen the marquees initially used as the passenger terminal. (Via Author)

The original control tower, seen from the north side spectators' enclosure. The signboard was the boarding point for the airport coach tours. (John Carter)

Beech C-45 YR-MIT in 1947 to 1948, with a
BOAC Liberator on the left of the photo. (Frank
Hudson)

In August 1946, BOAC's Advertising Controller wrote to the airline's Chairman and
Commercial Director regarding the possible public relations value of some better facilities for the increasing number of spectators at the airport. He suggested the provision
of electric signboards and special drive-in points for spectators, and requested that the
Ministry of Civil Aviation be approached to take some action. That same month the
ever-present spectre of a collision raised its head again when a BOAC York was involved
in a near-miss at the airport. It was positioning in from Hurn in low cloud and poor visibility. At the same time, a Douglas DC-4 of the Venezualan airline LAV was approaching
the airport as part of a promotional tour to publicise the airline's proposed new scheduled service to Europe. The control tower was unable to contact this aircraft as its radio
was tuned to the wrong frequency. The BOAC pilot received a number of warnings
about the LAV aircraft in the vicinity, and after red flares were fired he initiated a go-
around, during which he narrowly missed the DC-4, which was landing downwind on
the same runway. On 2 September 1946, BSAA inaugurated another new service across
the South Atlantic, this time a fortnightly Lancastrian schedule to Caracas via the Azores,
Bermuda and Jamaica. Also in September 1946, Trans-Canada Air Lines extended its
daily Montreal-Prestwick service through to London. The service had been operating
to Prestwick since July 1943 and used Avro Lancaster XPPs, a Canadian-built version
of the Lancaster B.X which outwardly resembled the Lancastrian. On 2 December
1946, Trans-Canada celebrated the completion of its 1,000th Atlantic crossing, and on
16 April 1947 the Lancasters were superseded by Canadair North Star airliners when
CF-TEM arrived at London with eighteen passengers.

On 19 September 1946 all three runways forming a triangular pattern at the airport were declared serviceable. Two were 6,000ft long and the other was 9,000ft, and
they were all 300ft wide. Runway 3, however, was still primarily reserved for aircraft
parking. In November 1946, two more airlines joined those serving London Airport
when Air France and Belgium's SABENA transferred their Paris and Brussels services
from Croydon. Most of the European airlines of the time were using Northolt, but the
Dakotas of Air France and SABENA were not equipped for Standard Beam Approaches

and so were not allowed to fly into that airport. In 1948, Air France was to introduce four-engined Sud Est Languedoc on the Paris service, and SABENA also later upgraded its equipment on the Brussels run to Douglas DC-4s and Convairs, although Dakotas continued to be used on Antwerp-London services. On 11 December 1946, the first scheduled all-cargo service arrived, a DC-4 of American Overseas Airlines carrying 9,000lb of fountain pens from the USA bound for Paris, and 3,000lb of relief supplies destined for Belgrade. That same month Pan American Airways inaugurated a New York-London-Paris passenger service with Constellation NC88833 *Clipper Polynesia*. During 1946, 63,151 passengers and 2,386 tons of cargo passed through London Airport aboard 2,046 flights serving eighteen destinations. As a portent for the future, the first complaints about aircraft noise were received from local residents.

5

NORTH SIDE EXPANSION

By the end of the year, the first prefabricated terminal buildings were ready to replace the marquees. Their design was inspired by similar terminals in use in the USA but they were constructed of materials used in post-war British prefabricated housing. They were single-storey structures with flat roofs, the walls being made of asbestos-based fibre panels held in place by a skeleton of preformed, reinforced concrete pillars. Once they were erected, salmon pink, biscuit beige and dove grey paintwork was applied to the interiors by the Ministry of Civil Aviation. The floors were made of concrete, covered with hundreds of square yards of carpeting. In December 1946, the Report of the London Airport Advisory Layout Panel was published. This panel had been appointed by the Ministry of Civil Aviation to consider and make recommendations as to the best layout for an international civil airport for London. Its terms of reference included the definition of the area available for use. The boundaries of the airport were defined thus: on the north side, the line proposed for the diverted Bath Road, which followed approximately the existing Cherry Lane, on the east side the River Crane, on the west side the Longford River and Harmondsworth village and on the south side, the Great South-West Staines reservoir. A permanent terminal building was to be erected in the centre of the hexagonal pattern formed by the intersection of six runways. The airport was to be developed in three stages: stage 1 – the completion of the RAF scheme for three runways, plus temporary buildings; stage 2 – a dual parallel runway system south of the Bath Road, plus completion of a large part of the Central Area apron and portions of the permanent terminal buildings, and lastly, stage 3 – extension of the main runway westwards and the construction of three more runways north of the Bath Road, together with connecting taxiways and increased facilities in the Central Area. The extension to the north of the Bath Road would threaten four schools, twelve pubs, a hospital, a police station and a greyhound stadium. In mid-December 1946, a Christmas party was given for 250 children of airport workers. The children stood on the tarmac to greet Father Christmas, who arrived on an Avro Lancastrian 'Christmas Special', carrying toys donated by the staff of the nine airlines using the airport. His somewhat premature arrival was attributed to 'tailwinds'.

On 4 January 1947, the first racehorse charter into the airport was operated by American Overseas Airlines DC-4 *Skyfreighter* N90421, carrying six horses from Los Angeles. On the following day, Skyways Avro Lancastrian G-AGLF *Sky Diplomat* departed on a marathon passenger charter to Hong Kong via Malta, Cairo, Karachi, Calcutta and Bangkok. The aircraft arrived back on the morning of 8 January. Another Skyways Lancastrian charter set off for Lydda in Palestine on 16 January, flying there and back direct with a turnaround of 1 hour, 30 minutes, and covering the 5,129 miles in a flying time of 22 hours, 27 minutes. On 18 January, British South American Airways, another Lancastrian operator, extended its Venezuala route along the west coast of South America to take in Lima and Santiago de Chile. Another active charter airline of the time was London Aero and Motor Services, using Handley Page Haltons. During one day in January, their Captain Theile took a service out of London at 2.00a.m., and landed at Vienna at 7.30a.m. Here, part of the load was taken off, and the aircraft continued onward to Belgrade, where the remainder of the cargo was offloaded. The aircraft then returned empty to London, arriving back at 8.00p.m. In March 1947, four LAMS Halton charters carried cargoes of vegetables into London from Tunis.

The new Avro Tudor airliner was intended to modernise BOAC's fleet and on 21 January 1947, HRH Princess Elizabeth named the BOAC Tudor 1 flagship G-AGRE *Elizabeth of England* in a ceremony at London Airport. She poured a flagon of Empire wine over the aircraft's nose and said: 'It gives me special pleasure to name this new aircraft for the peace-time service of civil aviation because it marks a landmark along the road away from war and destruction. I name this aircraft *Elizabeth of England*, may good fortune attend her wherever she may fly.' She then inspected the aircraft, accompanied by Sir Roy Dobson, Managing Director of A.V. Roe, and the Chairman of BOAC. However, after a protracted development and demands for countless modifications by the airline, the Tudor never eventually entered BOAC service. Early in 1947, a bizarre and tragic event took place at the airport. A nervous foreign passenger who had just arrived was closely questioned by customs officers who wanted to know how long he intended to stay, and whether he carried enough funds to support himself during his stay. They also asked to see his return ticket. The man became clearly distressed and escaped onto the apron, where, in front of scores of passengers, he ran into the revolving propellers of an aircraft about to depart and was killed. By March 1947, BOAC were operating thirty-four round-trips from London each week. They had more than 650 staff based there under the supervision of Station Superintendent G.R. (Jerry) Hawtin, who had previously held the same post at Hurn. The Mail Section handled 40 tons of mail each week plus diplomatic mail and was under the control of Station Officer D.G. Caldicott, who had previously worked at Croydon for thirteen years before the war and later at Hurn. The operating base for BOAC's new Halton fleet was transferred from Bovingdon that year and by the end of May 1947, nine examples were ready for service. After a proving flight to Colombo in April, the type took over the London-Cairo route on 2 June. They were placed onto the London-Colombo route in July, but from February 1948, they began to be supplanted by Avro Yorks, and G-AHDX flew the last BOAC Halton schedule on 3 May 1948, from Accra to London. On 15 April 1947, BOAC commenced commercial operations to

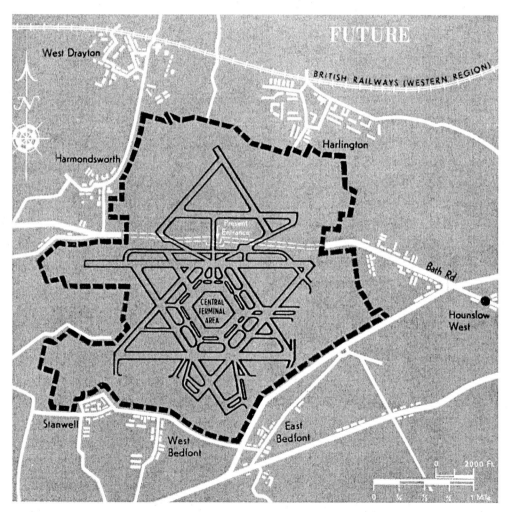

An extract from a 1948 MCA guidebook to London Airport, showing the planned runway layout including the runways to the north of the Bath Road. (Via Author)

1948 advertisement for FAMA Argentine International Airways. (Via Author)

Canada. A weekly Constellation service routed via Shannon (later changed to Prestwick) and Gander, configured to carry twenty-eight to thirty passengers plus cargo and mail. The westbound journey took 19 hours, 30 minutes and the round-trip fare was £139 11s.

On 25 April 1947, the passenger terminal finally acquired a fully licensed bar, operated by the catering division of Airwork Ltd, and during that month the first International Air Ball was held at London Airport. The Airport Manager had decided that the first such event should take place at the airport, rather than in London's West End. Cars were parked with the aid of mobile floodlights and during pauses in the music the sound of aircraft engines running up could be plainly heard. The new departure lounge was used as the ballroom and nearly 700 guests wearing a variety of uniforms and civilian dress ranging from white tie and tails to flannels attended. The VIP guests included the Minister of Civil Aviation, Lord Nathan.

1948 advertisement for Trans–Canada Air Lines. (Via Author)

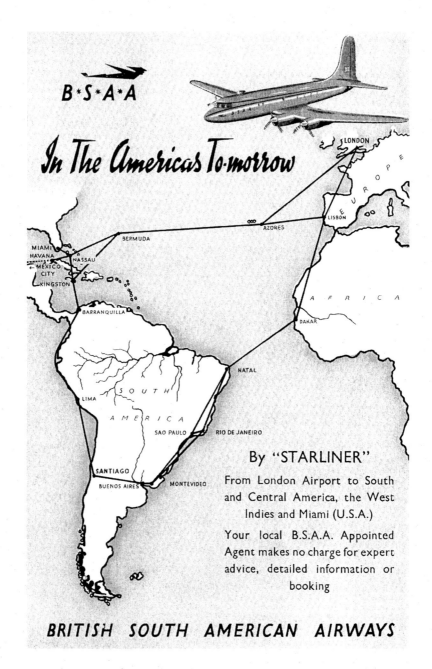

1948 advertisement for British South American Airways. (Via Author)

KLM DC-8 PH-DCC on the north side apron, surrounded by period vehicles. In front of the nose is the statue of Alcock and Brown. (Frank Hudson via airliners.net)

A KLM DC-7F freighter taxies in to the north side apron. (Frank Hudson via airliners.net)

Trans Atlantica Argentina *Star Liner* LV-GLH on the north side apron. Note the absence of security barriers, fences etc. (Frank Hudson via airliners.net).

The rare Boeing YC-97J Stratofreighter N9540C graces the north side tarmac. (Frank Hudson via airliners.net)

Island Air Services Rapide G-AGZO about to taxi out from the public enclosure for yet another pleasure flight in 1956. (Mick West via airliners.net)

In the early post-war years, the lack of positive air traffic control in the vicinity of the airport became apparent. All incoming flights (including those bound for Northolt) were handled by Uxbridge Area Control using wireless telegraphy from the time they crossed the English coast until they were handed over to Heathrow Tower, when only a few miles from the runway. Final landing clearances were passed to Heathrow Tower by telephone. This led to several incidents. In May 1947, Captain Tiller was inbound to London Airport in a BOAC Avro York. Just after he touched down, an Avro Anson was sighted flying downwind towards him a few feet above the runway. When he reported this to the control tower he was told that it was quite OK as the Anson was only practising approaches and was not landing.

During the year, GCA talk-down staff began to arrive at the airport in preparation for the introduction of Ground Controlled Approach procedures. Their equipment was mounted on a truck which could be positioned at the end of the runway in use. The facility was normally only intended for use in poor visibility, but the controllers often received requests for practice approaches in good weather. One frequent user was the Dutch airline KLM. When it was learnt that the airline had just carried out the 5,000th GCA approach at the airport, their staff presented the controllers with an iced cake decorated with a miniature runway and a man with a megaphone representing the 'talk-down'. Around this time there was a story going around about an Air France Dakota which landed safely on runway 28L after a night GCA approach in thick fog. At somewhere around Block 85 it allegedly departed the runway onto the grass, went around to the south of the GCA truck located in grass area 16, and found its way back onto the runway at Block 83. Nothing was known of this excursion until early the next morning when inspection teams found the tyre tracks on the grass. On 1 July 1947, the MCA took over complete control of the GCA equipment, until then operated by RAF personnel. Initially the MCA staff were still trained by the RAF, but on 27 October 1947, the MCA opened its own GCA Training School at Aldermaston. There were still complaints from pilots about the length of time taken to issue landing clearances, especially in poor visibility. On 19 November 1947, BOAC Dakota G-AGKE under the command of Captain Walbran arrived overhead London Airport and was advised that the flight was number four in the queue to land. After 1 hour, 2 minutes, the captain was finally given clearance to land, spotting the runway when 50ft from its near end. In an attempt to resolve the problems occurring between pilots and controllers, the experienced BOAC pilot Captain Alcock was appointed Liason Officer with the MCA staff at the airport in November 1947.

In the meantime, new services continued to be introduced and more notable 'one-off' flights were made. On 30 April 1947, an RAF Mosquito PR34 departed the airport for Cape Town at 6.04p.m., arriving there via fuel stops at El Adem and Kisumu in a total flight time of 21 hours, 31 minutes. Pan-American Airways introduced New York-London all-cargo DC-4 services on 5 May, and seventeen days later inaugurated Dakota feeder services to Vienna, Brussels, Frankfurt and Prague to connect with transatlantic schedules. Also in May BOAC re-opened its weekly Dakota service to Lydda, with a nightstop in Malta en route. On 28 May, BSAA began a series of experimental non-stop flights to Bermuda utilising in-flight refuelling. The aircraft was refuelled en route by a Lancaster tanker based in the Azores, enabling the initial flight of some 4,000 miles to be completed in around twenty hours. During May 1947, some 20,000 passengers passed through London Airport. BOAC and BSAA operated 205 inbound services and 179 departures, carrying almost 4,500 passengers. To cater for the ever-growing public interest in the comings and goings, a new public enclosure near to the control tower and north of the north taxiway was opened on 1 June 1947. A running commentary on the aircraft movements, interspersed with music, was broadcast over loudspeakers, and on the first day an estimated 3,000 visitors paid their 3d for admission plus 1s for car parking. The Mayor and Mayoress of Hounslow were among the local dignitaries present, all of whom were given pleasure flights in a BOAC York. The enclosure was open on weekdays from 2.00p.m. until 9.00p.m., and at weekends and on public holidays from 11.00a.m. until 9.00p.m. Pleasure flights in small aircraft were on offer, and during June, 52,606 people paid for admission. The total revenue, including car parking charges, amounted to more than £900. This enclosure was to remain open until 1953, when the closure of runway 28R for construction of the new tunnel into the Central Area led to the relocation of the public enclosure to an area between the taxiway and

BOAC Britannia 102 G-ANBG alongside a Pan American Airways DC-7C on the north side apron in 1957. (Mick West via airliners.net).

An Air France Languedoc taxies out from the north side apron on 2 May 1952. (Frank Hudson via airliners.net)

Trans World Airlines DC-4 freighter N45343 on the north side tarmac in 1955. (Frank Hudson via airliners.net)

El Al Constellation 4X-AKA on the north side in 1950 (Frank Hudson via airliners.net)

Royal Canadian Air Force Canadair C-5, serial number 10000, on the north side after a VIP flight for the funeral of HM King George VI in February 1952. (Frank Hudson via airliners.net)

Howard Super Ventura N9060, a rare executive visitor to the north side apron on 14 June 1958. (Frank Hudson via airliners.net)

BSAA Lancaster freighter G–AGUM and a QANTAS Constellation on the north side during 1949.
(Frank Hudson via airliners.net)

The Monsanto Chemical Company's Consolidated Canso N5904N on the north side apron in August
1955. (Frank Hudson via airliners.net)

BOAC Stratocruiser G-AKGJ in the original natural metal livery in 1950. (Frank Hudson via airliners.net)

American Overseas Airlines Stratocruiser N90948 on 16 July 1950. (Frank Hudson via airliners.net)

the closed runway. Access to the new enclosure was by foot from the site of the original one, with escorts being provided for the crossing of the live north taxiway.

By June 1947, the first triangle of runways was operational. Runway No.1 was 3,000yds long and the other two measured 2,000yds. Runway No.4 was complete, and work had commenced on Runway No.5. The Airport Manager was Roger Pugh, who was responsible for the MCA operations and a staff of around 400. On 14 June 1947 the total staff at the airport numbered 851, a 73 per cent increase on August 1946. The BOAC Passenger Arrivals staff numbered twenty-one, consisting of five Station Assistants and sixteen Station Clerks. They were divided into three teams of six staff, to provide twenty-hour cover and an overlap during the period 1.00-3.00p.m. The Passenger Arrivals Section was later combined with the Aircraft Arrivals Section, whose duties included unloading the aircraft and checking and distributing all traffic documents. The Passenger Departures Section was likewise combined with Service Control, which was responsible for the production of all load and trim sheets and for supervision of the loading of the aircraft. At the time the Passenger Departures staff numbered twenty, comprising a Station Officer, three Station Assistants and sixteen Station Clerks. There was also a third section called Enquiries which dealt with passenger queries, aircraft movement information, ticket issue, and mishandled loads. A working party of the time recommended that to avoid the need for a member of the passenger handling team to meet incoming flights, the aircraft's steward or stewardess should escort the passengers to the arrivals area. This was considered important because 'passengers have become accustomed to the steward during the flight'.

On 5 June 1947, Handley Page Halifax G-AIHW of the Lancashire Aircraft Corporation, inbound from Valencia with a cargo of apricots, made a heavy landing at the airport and was written off, the wireless operator sustaining slight injuries. On 18 June Pan American Constellation NC86520 *Clipper America* passed through on the airline's first round-the-world service. This was flown weekly and brought the weekly total of Pan American services through the airport to fourteen. 23 July saw the first visit of a Douglas DC-6, when SABENA's OO-AWA flew Brussels-London-Copenhagen and back, and carried out a local flight during its stopover in London. Two days later there was another landing incident when a Skyways Avro York carrying seventeen passengers and seven crew from Moscow via Berlin overran the runway, continued onward over hard turf, a ditch and a concrete road, and came to rest astride the Duke of Northumberland River. On the evening of 7 August, the experimental Avro Tudor VII, fitted with Bristol Hercules engines in place of the usual Rolls-Royce Merlins, visited London Airport and gave a demonstration flight of some 40 minutes' duration to the south coast and back, circling Brighton before returning. In August HM the Queen paid her first visit when she arrived from Yorkshire in a Viking of the King's Flight. During that month BOAC inaugurated a weekly Dakota service to Teheran which entailed

Trans World Airlines Super Constellation N101R on the north side in 1958. (Frank Hudson via airliners.net)

TWA Super Constellation N7109C being serviced on the north side apron in 1956. (Frank Hudson via airliners.net)

two overnight stops on the multi-leg journey. On 30 September, BSAA Avro Tudor G-AHNK *Star Lion* set off on yet another proving flight to South America which led to the introduction of the type on scheduled services to Havana via Lisbon, the Azores, Bermuda and Nassau on 31 October. During the summer of 1947 over 130,000 passed through the airport and larger airliners were soon brought into service to cope with the continually growing demand for seats. On 3 November, Aer Lingus introduced fifty-eight-seat *Constellations* on its 'Silver Shamrock' service from Dublin, and in December QANTAS began using its own new Constellations on through services from Sydney.

Early in 1948, the MCA carried out more trials to investigate the feasibility of using mid-air refuelling to permit the operation of non-stop transatlantic services. During the period 4 February-28 May BOAC operated weekly non-stop cargo services between London and Montreal with Liberator G-AHYD, which was refuelled en route by Lancastrian tankers of Flight Refuelling operating out of Shannon and Gander. Tragedy struck on 2 March 1948 when SABENA Dakota OO-AWH crashed onto runway 10L after completing a ground-controlled approach in 200yds visibility. The aircraft was inbound from Brussels. All three crew members and seventeen of the nineteen passengers were killed.

In April 1948 Wing Commander Snowball of BSAA was sent a letter by the MCA offering the airline the use of a cottage at the airport formerly used by the building contractor Wimpey as a welfare office. BSAA decided it could make use of the cottage

SABENA DC-6B OO-SDG on a rainswept north side apron. (SABENA)

as office space and by their duty engineer, but as it was gas-lit and had no electricity they asked for a supply to be laid on. At that time their pilot training office was in Hut 47. The Training Captain was Captain E.E. (Rod) Rodley DSO DFC AFC, and the Deputy Training Captain was Frank Taylor, later to move on to the BOAC Argonaut fleet and be selected as one of the captains to fly the Queen Mother and Princess Margaret to South Africa. BSAA's Navigation Captain was Captain R.C. Alabaster DSO DFC. On 17 April 1948 their Tudor IV *Star Panther* carried a group of company directors on a trade mission to South America at a time when the type was grounded for normal scheduled services following the unexplained disappearance of a BSAA example. The chartered aircraft returned safely to London on 9 May. In July 1948, BSAA passed on to the MCA the contents of a letter of complaint from a London businessman who had been meeting and seeing off clients at the airport for some months and was annoyed at the lack of passenger facilities. Among the points he made were: there was no bar in the arrivals shed, and the bar in the departure area could not be accessed by arriving passengers; the 'canteen' (in actuality one trestle table) in the arrivals shed served only tea, which most American passengers did not like. There was no single building which served as a central enquiry point for all the airlines; the airline buildings were dispersed and inadequately signposted, so it was hard to tell if a building belonged to a airline or the airport administration; the only easy access to the outside grass waiting area was over a temporary path of planks surrounded by pickaxes, dust and broken concrete,;the rear entrance to the arrivals shed was locked for no apparent reason. BSAA had replied to the complaints, saying that both themselves and BOAC were at loggerheads with the MCA over the issues and that they were of the opinion that Airwork should be put in charge of all catering at the airport as they always seemed to be able to supply their passengers with food and drink in the departures waiting area.

Foreign royalty passed through the airport on 1 June 1948 when Emir Faisal of Saudi Arabia arrived from New York aboard BOAC Constellation G-AKCE and was accorded a guard of honour from the Sixth Airborne Division. On 8 June Air India International became the first Asian airline to operate scheduled services to the UK when it opened a Bombay-Cairo-Geneva-London route. The weekly service used Constellations and was scheduled to take under 24 hours in each direction, making it the fastest service from England to India. In 1948, the airlines serving London on a scheduled basis and their aircraft comprised: BOAC (York, Dakota, Liberator, Constellation, Lancastrian freighter) KLM (DC-4, Dakota), SABENA (Dakota), Air France (Languedoc), Pan American Airways (Constellation, Dakota, DC-4 freighter), Trans Canada Air Lines (Canadair North Star), British South American Airways (York, Lancastrian), Czechoslovakian State Airlines (Dakota), American Overseas Airlines (Constellation, DC-4), South African Airways (DC-4), QANTAS (Constellation), Air India (Constellation), Iberia (DC-4) Skyways (DC-4), FAMA (York, DC-4).

For the summer of 1948, spectators could avail themselves of conducted coach tours of the airport which started out from outside the control tower and went around the parking apron and the BOAC hangars. At weekends a large airliner such as a Constellation or DC-4 was often parked close to the public enclosure and the public were shown over it. During

Pan American DC-6B N6529C *Clipper Fidelity* on the north side apron. (Air-Britain)

RAF Transport Command Britannia XN398 waits on the north side as a Bristol Sycamore helicopter brings in its VIP passenger on 28 June 1961. To the left of the Britannia's tail is the Alcock and Brown statue. (Via Author)

the afternoons, gramophone records were played between the commentator's announcements, and, occasionally messages between the control tower and aircraft were relayed over the loudspeakers. The enclosure contained a tea pavilion and for the children there was a sandpit and Shetland ponies to ride. From 25 April 1948, Island Air Services operated

BKS Air Transport Britannia G–AND in the long-term parking area on the north side. (Air-Britain)

Skyways of London Hermes G–ALDE on the north side. (Air-Britain)

A Stratocruiser and a Hermes of BOAC share the north side apron. (Via Author)

7 February 1952. HM Queen Elizabeth II arrives aboard a BOAC Argonaut and descends the steps to set foot on English soil for the first time as monarch. (Heathrow Airport plc)

An early line up on the north side, comprising BOAC Constellation G-AHEL, a BOAC Lancastrian and an RAF York. (Michael H. Starritt)

pleasure flights with de Havilland Rapide biplanes on Sunday afternoons. A fifteen-minute flight cost £1, and demand was so great that at the peak of the season four Rapides were in service, backed up by aircraft such as Airspeed Consuls hired from other operators. A typical Rapide flight went to Hyde Park and back, while the Consul usually flew as far as the Tower of London. Island Air Services had the sole concession for pleasure flights from the airport and by the mid-1950s they were carrying out over 100 flights each day between the hours of 10a.m. and dusk. The company suffered a mishap on 1 August 1952 when Rapide G-ALBB was approaching runway 23L at the conclusion of yet another pleasure flight. The aircraft ahead of it on the approach was a Boeing Stratocruiser, and the Rapide encountered its wake turbulence at 300ft. It went out of control and crashed just inside the airport boundary, 475yds from the runway threshold. The pilot was severely injured and five out of the eight passengers suffered minor injuries. By 1955, the scheduled traffic at the airport included such large types as the Douglas DC-6, Stratocruiser and Super Constellation, and in answer to questions in Parliament the Parliamentary Secretary to the Ministry of Transport and Civil Aviation, Mr John Profumo, announced that owing to the increase in air traffic and the complexity of air traffic control the MTCA had decided that pleasure flying at London Airport must come to an end.

In 1948 the air traffic control procedures were as follows: aircraft using the Metropolitan Control Zone, including those flying to/from Northolt, were directed through three entry/exit points for London Airport. Through the Gravesend 'gate' went KLM to Amsterdam, SABENA to Brussels and Antwerp, American Overseas Airlines to Frankfurt, SAS to Stockholm, Pan American Airways to Germany, and BEA and Air France to Paris. The Dunsfold 'gate' was used by BOAC Yorks going to South Africa and the east, BSAA to Lisbon en route to South America, Pan American to Istanbul, South African Airways to Johannesburg, and aircraft of Panair do Brasil, QANTAS, Swissair and Air India. All transatlantic traffic went through the Woodley 'gate'. At times of congestion incoming flights were 'stacked' vertically. The 500ft height separation employed was much criticised as inadequate, and on 4 July a DC-6 of Scandinavian Airlines System and an RAF Transport Command Avro York collided near Northolt while the DC-6 was attempting to leave the stack to return to Amsterdam. All thirty-nine people aboard both aircraft lost their lives.

July 1948 saw two unusual flights. A BOAC Lancastrian freighter carried two consignments of 'Zube' cough lozenges, totalling some five million lozenges and weighing 3.5 tons, to Johannesburg. On 25 July, the experimental jet-powered Vickers Nene-Viking flew to Villacoublay airfield near Paris in 34 minutes, 7 seconds at an average speed of 384mph. That month saw the inaugural meeting of the London (Heathrow) Airport Consultative Committee, the first, and for some years the only, such committee in the UK. In August 1948 the report of the Select Committee on Estimates for the Construction of London Airport was published. It stated that the present temporary terminal buildings would be superseded by semi-permanent buildings in the Central Area. These would be two-storey pre-fabricated structures, and their erection would be used to gain experience of the requirements for a major civil airport. They would not interfere with the permanent buildings to be erected later, and the experience gained would allow construction of the permanent buildings to be completed more quickly. Once stage 2 of the airport, with six runways in operation, was completed, the maximum capacity should be seventy-two aircraft movements per hour. The construction of the last three runways, on the north side of the Bath Road, under Stage 3 would involve diverting the Bath Road some distance to the north, and as alternative accommodation for the occupants of the houses to be demolished would have to be provided first, the runways could not be completed for a number of years. The total cost was shown in the Estimates as a provisional figure of £26 million. In August 1948, eight Dictaphone Belt Recorders/Reproducers were installed at London Airport, along with a further eight at Northolt. These recorded and logged all radio conversations between aircraft and the airport.

On 15 October 1948, an International Ball was held at the airport. The entire Departure Section of the Passenger Handling Block was taken over for the ball, and from 2.00p.m. that day, departing passengers were routed through one side of the Arrivals Block. Around 500 guests enjoyed the evening, which was organised by the various airport authorities including Health, Customs and the MTCA. The guests were received by Sir John and Lady D'Albiac. The period from 27 November–2 December 1948 saw the longest period

BOAC Stratocruiser G-ANTY is towed across the north side while on lease to Nigeria Airways. (Air-Britain)

of disruption due to fog experienced up till then in British civil aviation history. Out of a total of seventy-three services scheduled, BOAC managed to operate fifty-nine, but only seven of these actually departed from London Airport. The rest flew out of Hurn, Prestwick, Southampton and RAF St Eval. Eighteen out of twenty KLM services from London were cancelled and arrangements made for the passengers to get to Holland by surface transport. 120 passengers were placed on the boat trains, and on 29 November, a party of seventy-four was escorted by a KLM representative on the sea crossing to the Hook of Holland. From there, sixty-two of them were taken by coach to Schipol Airport to catch onward long-haul flights. During 1948, 16,764 landings and 16,791 take-offs were recorded, but despite this growth the airport still retained an air of intimacy and in January 1949 it still only took 10 minutes for arriving passengers to pass between the immigration and currency control officials seated on their stools. They were then invited to leave the building via a small door in the wall behind the officials' desks, and on doing so they found themselves in a tiny car park directly adjoining the Bath Road.

BSAA suffered a major blow on 17 January 1949 when their Avro Tudor 4 G-AGRE *Star Ariel* disappeared somewhere between Bermuda and Jamaica. This was the second BSAA Tudor to vanish on a scheduled service and the type was then grounded by the authorities. The subsequent aircraft shortage led to the merger of BSAA into BOAC on 30 July 1949. BSAA traffic staff were absorbed into various locations around the BOAC network and a few of them were posted to the BOAC Service Control Section at London Airport. This section was staffed by a mixture of ex-RAF aircrew, former Imperia Airways personnel, and some who had previously worked for BOAC in the Middle East and elsewhere during the Second World War. The main duties of the section included the preparation of aircraft load sheets, and passenger and crew manifests. By 1949, BEA was running out of space at Northolt and had taken the decision to transfer operations to London Airport as soon as possible. In May, the airline announced that its new fleet of 'Elizabethan' class Airspeed Ambassadors would be based there in a new maintenance base to be constructed to house them. At the beginning of April, the giant Boeing Stratocruiser paid its first visit to the airport when Pan American's N1028V *Clipper Flying Cloud* arrived on a proving flight from Gander via Shannon. It carried seventeen crew members (many of them supernumeraries) and forty passengers including Willis G. Lipscomb, Vice-President Traffic and Sales. During its time at the airport the public were permitted to inspect the aircraft, and it carried many journalists, travel agents and other guests on demonstration flights. The proving flight was followed in due course by the inaugural Pan-American scheduled service from New York on 1 June.

On 23 July, American Overseas Airlines also brought their Stratocruiser *Flagship Great Britain* into London Airport for a series of demonstration flights over southern England. Another unusual aircraft type flew into the airport on 11 May 1949 when Hawker test pilot Neville Duke positioned the second prototype Hawker Fury fighter monoplane in from the factory airfield at Langley. An hour before dawn on the following day, he took off to deliver the aircraft to the Pakistan Air Force, flying first of all to Rome and breaking the London-Rome speed record previously held by a Vampire jet.

1949 saw the beginning of preparations for scheduled passenger services by the revolutionary de Havilland Comet jet airliner. On 22 October, the prototype G-ALVG was flown into London Airport for trials that established that it could use current approach and landing patterns without causing disruption. Two days later it was back at the airport preparing to fly to Castel Benito in Libya for 'hot and high' trials. On 28 October,

Two generations: BOAC Comet 4 G-APDE and Stratocruiser G-ANTY on the north side apron. (British Aerospace plc)

Passengers board BOAC Comet 1 G-ALYP bound for Johannesburg on the inaugural commercial jet passenger service on 2 May 1952. (British Aerospace plc)

Passengers leave their BOAC coach on the north side and board Comet 4 G-APDE for a service to New York on 14 November 1958. (British Aerospace plc)

The scene on the north side apron on 2 May 1952, as passengers prepare to board BOAC Comet 1 G-ALYP on the inaugural jet service. (British Aerospace plc)

A Yugoslavian Dakota outside the north side terminal buildings on 30 August 1952. (Peter Maddocks)

TWA Super Constellation N7106C takes on catering supplies on the north side apron. (Malcolm D. Stride)

Grumman Mallard amphibian NC2956 took off from London but lost height when about 50ft above the runway. The undercarriage struck the grass and the aircraft then continued across the airfield a few feet above the ground before crashing and bursting into flames. The captain, radio officer and four passengers were killed and the engineer officer survived with injuries. During November 1949, BOAC introduced Canadair Argonauts on its routes to Cairo, Kuwait, Abadan and Singapore, followed by Boeing Stratocruisers on the route to New York via Prestwick on 6 December. To assist with airport identification, two new beacons were installed in December, a green identification beacon flashing 'VA' in morse, and an alternating white/green airport location beacon situated in Heston, about a mile and a half from the airport.

In late 1949, the landing fees at the airport were the subject of discussion by the MCA Committee on Public Accounts. It was revealed that the landing fee for a Constellation arriving from the USA was £20 12s 6d, compared to £12 14s 9d at Brussels and £4 12s 0d at Paris. By late December, the second stage of construction at the airport was at an advanced stage. Runways 1 and 2 of the original RAF triangular layout were in service, together with Runway 6, which became operational in June to replace Runway 3 which was already being broken up. Construction of a fourth runway (Runway 7) had been found to be necessary in order to clear the future Central Area, across which Runway 3 had stretched. During the late 1940s and early 1950s there was a small café called Ben's just outside the Bath Road entrance. It consisted of an old lean-to building with a marquee extension, and was originally a café for lorry drivers using the Bath Road. It was to be demolished during the construction of the tunnel into the Central Area. On the other side of the road was the Heathrow Restaurant, a chintzy tearoom which served shepherd's pie and two veg, sausage and mash, and other delights. Along the Bath Road were three pubs: The Bricklayers Arms (later The Air Hostess), The Three Magpies and The Old Magpies. Just inside the airport boundary Airwork operated a snack bar adjacent to the passenger terminal and also opened the first Green Dragon Café. This comprised one half of a large green corrugated building, the other half of which served as the export cargo bonded warehouse. It provided teas and snacks for the airport workers and was later to become a press conference room for VIPs passing through the airport. By 1950, there was also an MCA canteen alongside the control tower. Between 1950 and 1955 the airport personnel office was a Nissen hut located on the Bath Road at Harlington Corner. There was also a hostel for female airport staff staying overnight.

From 16 April 1950, two of BEA's hourly services to Paris operated from London Airport instead of Northolt. At the time they were the only BEA services from the airport and the flights were handled by BOAC. It would be April 1951 before BEA established its own handling unit at London Airport but once it was operational BEA earned useful revenue by handling the flights of its European rivals, who had also begun to transfer their services over from Northolt. On 18 April 1950, the Argentinian airline FAMA reduced its London-Buenos Aires journey time to 34 hours, 10 minutes with the introduction of Douglas DC-6Bs which routed via Lisbon, Dakar, Natal and Rio de Janeiro. By May, plans were being made to increase the capacity of the existing terminal buildings to cope with the expected heavy increase in traffic the following year. The intention was to provide an additional channel in both the arrival and departure halls

The Bristol Brabazon prototype during one of its visits to the airport. (Mick West)

so that a greater number of flights could be handled simultaneously. Also planned was a £5,000 RSPCA scheme to provide facilities for animals passing through the airport. At the time an average of 300 monkeys alone arrived each week, and animals were often left aboard aircraft overnight as there were no quarantine facilities at the airport. The prototype of the mighty Bristol Brabazon airliner paid its first visit to the airport on 15 June 1950 and was inspected by Mr Strauss (Minister of Supply) and Lord Pakenham (Minister of Civil Aviation). That evening more than 4,000 people paid 6d to enter the public enclosure and then queued to pay a further 1s for seats in coaches which were allowed to approach to within 50ft of the floodlit Brabazon, which was guarded by forty-nine policemen. The next day, Bristol Chief Test Pilot 'Bill' Pegg took it up for two local flights before returning it to Filton. The airport authorities were anticipating some 50,000 people to turn up to watch these flights but in the event only 13,361 did so. The Brabazon returned in July 1951 for more demonstration flights but was never accepted by its intended operator BOAC and the prototype was eventually broken up. One type that did join BOAC was the Handley Page Hermes, the first British post-war airliner to enter service. The flagship of the BOAC fleet, G-ALDI, was named *Hannibal* by Lord Pakenham at London Airport on 11 July 1950. South African wine was poured over the nose to christen it, and demonstration flights were laid on for the guests who included officials of the various Ministries and BOAC. In command of the flights was Captain ASM Rendall, who had served as First Officer on the original *Hannibal*, an HP42 biplane airliner of Imperial Airways.

Close-up of a BOAC Argonaut taken through the window of the airport tour coach. (John Carter)

BOAC Comet 1 G-ALYP, later to be lost in a mid-air break-up. (John Carter)

On 6 July 1950, Minister of Civil Aviation Lord Pakenham announced that important changes had been made to the plans for the Central Area terminal buildings.
Until then it had been the intention to erect temporary buildings to serve until the
final design of the permanent buildings had been decided by an architectural competition. However, space constraints in the Central Area had now made this impractical
and the interim buildings would not now be constructed. Frederick Gibberd CBE
FRIBA AMTPI, the consulting architect for the temporary buildings, was appointed
architect for the new permanent terminal buildings and control tower to be sited in
the Central Area. American Overseas Airlines operated its final service from London
Airport on 25 September 1950. Its New York-London route then passed to Trans
World Airlines as part of a route-swap deal and at the end of the month TWA began
Constellation services New York-London-Frankfurt, the airline's first services through
London. On 31 October 1950, BEA Viking G-AHPN crashed at the airport with the
loss of twenty-eight of its thirty occupants. The aircraft was on a service from Paris
(Le Bourget) to Northolt, but diverted to London Airport because of fog. The crew
carried out a ground controlled approach to runway 28R, which also had poor visibility. They announced that they were overshooting, but then struck the runway with
the undercarriage retracted. The Viking bounced back into the air before impacting
the runway again, and coming to rest alongside a pile of drainpipes and bursting into
flames. Because of the dense fog it took the fire crews between 5 and 10 minutes
to locate the crash site. An aviation era came to an end on 7 November 1950 when
BOAC replaced its last flying-boat service, from Southampton to Johannesburg, with
a three-times-weekly Hermes operation from London Airport via Tripoli, Kano,
Brazzaville and Livingstone.

Aerolineas Argentinas Comet 4 LV-AHN on the north side in November 1959. (Clive Dyball)

In 1950, London Airport handled a total of 523,000 passengers. This was to increase to 796,092 in 1951, 861,000 in 1952 and 1.205 million in 1953. These increases reflected the transfer of BEA's operations from Northolt, but an article in the 28 September 1950 issue of *Flight* magazine expressed concern over the effect such a move would have on surface travel to and from the airport, saying once Northolt traffic moves to London Airport.

It has been calculated that there will be an almost continuous convoy of coaches between Heathrow and the coach terminal, with only three minutes between vehicles in each direction. Under daylight conditions the time taken from Airways Terminal at Victoria to Heathrow is about fifty minutes. At night it may only be thirty-five minutes. One of the great advantages of Northolt is that there is a fast run from Kensington Air Station to the airport, with, as a rule, only a slight traffic hold-up at Shepherd's Bush. The run between Kensington Air Station and Northolt seldom takes more than thirty minutes, even in the daytime. But there is always, during the day, a hold-up at Hammersmith Broadway, and when coming from Heathrow to London there is a very slow, narrow, congested one-way system when approaching Hammersmith. That confusion will not only be worse con-founded, but complete chaos will be caused to traffic in both directions when coaches are on the road at 3 minute intervals. There could be four solutions. The first would be the provision of an extra track each way on the existing electric railway between Hounslow West and Hammersmith, with an extension from Hounslow to Heathrow… The second would be the building of a completely new road, with expensive flyovers, from Chiswick to central London, and the possible widening of the Great West Road. The third would be some sort of overhead rope-railway, and the fourth would be the use of helicopters as

Upper: BOAC Dakota G-AGKK by the spectators enclosure in the early 1950s. *Lower:* KLM Convair 340 PH-TEK seen from the spectators' enclosure.

Seaboard and Western Super Constellation N6504C taxies past the mobile GCA installation in November 1959. (Clive Dyball)

A series of postcard views of the spectators' enclosure on the north side in the early 1950s. (Via John Carter)

The view from the relocated spectators' enclosure on the north side in the 1950s. Nearest the camera are DC-4s of SAS and Iberia. (John Carter)

airport coaches…the thought of a stream of helicopters, one every three minutes in each direction, is not a very pleasant prospect to contemplate, especially in bad weather.

On 1 March 1951, BOAC used its spacious new Boeing Stratocruisers to inaugurate the 'Monarch' deluxe service between London and New York. Passengers had to pay a surcharge on the normal fare and in return they were treated to VIP service. Free cocktails and champagne were served as aperitifs to a gourmet dinner of caviar, turtle soup, salmon, chicken, strawberries and cream. The service initially operated on three days each week but was upgraded to a daily basis from 1 May. The Stratocruisers had insufficient range for non-stop flights to New York against the prevailing winds, so a refuelling stop was made at Gander on the westbound leg. These were busy days for BOAC as on 22 March the second prototype Comet jet airliner was handed over to them and on 24 May the BOAC Comet Unit began a series of twelve overseas route-proving flights over the course of that year. These culminated in a London-Cairo-Karachi-Bangkok-Singapore-Bangkok-Calcutta-Karachi-Basra-Cairo-Rome-London trip during the period 10-18 October. TWA's response to BOAC's 'Monarch' service to New York was their 'London Ambassador' service using Constellations in an eighteen-berth sleeper layout, and Pan American also inaugurated its own 'President' and 'President Special' deluxe Stratocruiser services. An article on the airport in the 17 February 1951 issue of *Picture Post* magazine stated that there were on average 125 movements each day by aircraft of twenty-one airlines.

Every day around 2,000 passengers and 30 tons of freight passed through, including many animals. The airport was run by the MCA which provided essential services. BOAC employed about 3,000 staff and handled around half of the foreign airlines using the airport. In 1951, KLM introduced new Foden air-conditioned 'two-tier' coaches on the run between the airport and their London town terminal in Sloane Street. Each coach was configured to carry the passenger load of a Convair 240 airliner, minus the ten per cent or so of passengers who travelled independently to the airport. They were operated for KLM by United Service Transport Ltd. About 1,500 men were permanently engaged on the airport expansion programme. Many were employed by the Air Ministry Works Directorate on behalf of the MCA, but there were also eighteen outside contractors. Experimental scheduled helicopter services between London Airport and Birmingham (Haymills Rotorstation) via Northolt were inaugurated by BEA with Sikorsky S-51s on 1 June 1951. This service was initially for invited guests, but from 4 June it became available to normal fare-paying passengers. Three round-trips were scheduled each day and by the time the service was terminated on 19 April 1952 it had carried 10,987 passengers at an average load factor of 58 per cent. On 3 September 1951, G-ALZN, on-loan from the manufacturer, operated BEA's first 'Elizabethan' class Airspeed Ambassador Service to Paris. It was substituted for Vikings until 18 September, by which time it had carried 314 fare-paying passengers. The late delivery of BEA's own fleet of Elizabethans caused scheduling problems, and some of their allocated services had to be operated by Vikings out of Northolt. Furthermore, if an Elizabethan service was overbooked it was necessary to substitute two Vikings. As these were still based at Northolt it meant that passengers had to be bussed between the two airports.

During 1951, a new two-storey reinforced concrete building was becoming visible on the north side apron. This would house airline offices and a new departure

Swiss Air Lines Convair
HB-IRS in the early 1950s.
(Frank Hudson)

lounge when BEA transferred its operations from Northolt. The contract had been awarded to the winner of a design competition between twenty contractors specialising in structural steel or reinforced concrete structures. There was as yet no sign of buildings in the Central Area, although excavations for the tunnel to carry road traffic under the number one runway were well advanced. The tunnel was to be 2,600ft-long, with 20ft-wide dual carriageways in each direction, permitting a traffic flow rate of 2,000 vehicles per hour. It was also to have cycle tracks and pedestrian walkways. Its shallow depth and the nature of the gravel subsoil precluded conventional boring, so it was built by the 'cut and cover' method. A huge trench was dug and a reinforced concrete shell was put in place before it was covered over. This shell was 86ft wide and 23ft high, sufficient for London Transport double-decker buses to pass through. Construction work, including a new public enclosure on top of the tunnel entrance in the Central Area, had been subject to hold-ups caused by a number of strikes. During 1950 around 340,000 spectators had visited the airport. On 8 October 1951, their Royal Highnesses Princess Elizabeth and HRH the Duke of Edinburgh flew from London to Montreal via Gander aboard BOAC Stratocruiser G-AKGK *Canopus*, commanded by Captain O.P. Jones. The flight was the first leg of their Canadian Tour, the first Royal Tour to set off from the United Kingdom by air. On 21 October the BOAC Comet Training Unit was transferred from Hatfield to London Airport. By the end of the year the Festival of Britain had helped to boost the annual passenger total to 796,092, aboard 49,341 aircraft movements. By the beginning of 1952 green centre line lighting had been installed on all taxiways except those to the

SABENA Dakota OO-AWZ seen from the Central Area spectators' enclosure in the 1950s. (John Carter)

Announcing

BEA

SILVER WING

A new Luxury Service between London and Paris

ON JUNE 9th BRITISH EUROPEAN AIRWAYS are to open a new luxury service named the Silver Wing, between London and Paris. The Silver Wing will leave London Airport daily at 1.00 p.m. and arrive at Le Bourget at 2.20 p.m.

On the return journey, it will leave Le Bourget at 12.30 p.m. and arrive at London Airport at 1.50 p.m. It will therefore be not

only the most luxurious, but also the fastest, of all daily services between the two capitals. Flying time is 80 minutes.

ONLY ELIZABETHAN AIRLINERS WILL FLY on the Silver Wing service. These magnificent aeroplanes cruise at 245 m.p.h., or just over four miles a minute. Their cabins are pressurized and kept at a

fresh and equable temperature. The Silver Wing will carry forty passengers, and a crew of six including a head steward, a bar steward and stewardess. The wide windows of the Elizabethan set *beneath* the high wings, give to every passenger splendid and panoramic views.

A CHAMPAGNE LUNCH WILL BE SERVED immediately after take-off. A typical Bill of Fare would include smoked Scottish salmon, grilled lamb cutlet and cape pears. The Silver Wing is the *only* air service between London and Paris

which offers a hot lunch. Complimentary Moët et Chandon special cuvée champagne will also be served. And the widest choice of duty-free drinks is available from the Elizabethan bar. This is one of the most luxurious ways of travelling in the world.

The Silver Wing is only one of BEA's many daily services to Paris and the Continent. The Silver Wing fare is the normal

£15 . 19 . 0 return fare. Other fares (depending on the time of departure and period of validity) are £12 . 15 . 0 and £10 . 10 . 0 return. Your Travel Agent or B.E.A. will give you full information and take your booking; or else apply direct to BEA, Dorland Hall, Regent St., London, S.W.1. (Telephone: GERrard 9833.)

BRITISH   EUROPEAN   AIRWAYS

A 1952 advertisement previewing the BEA Silver Wing luxury service to Paris. (Via Author)

north of runway 28R/10L, where the blue taxiway edge lighting remained. The passenger terminals were reaching the limits of their capacity but the MCA was reluctant to initiate construction of further buildings on the north side site because of the planned transfer of all passenger and air traffic control facilities to the 54-acre Central Area site. Two main passenger buildings were planned there, one for European routes and one for long-haul services. A new public enclosure was to be sited on top of the short-haul terminal. In November the MCA received proposals for the installation of FIDO (Fog, Intensive Dispersal Of) at the airport. Statistics for 1951 had shown 116 flight cancellations outbound and 126 inbound, of which sixty-five and seventy-five respectively were thought to have been avoidable if FIDO had been installed. The system was also thought to have been capable of eliminating seventy-four out of the ninety-four diversions caused by bad weather, and 140 out of the 178 delays requiring overnight stops. It was proposed that a 3,950ft length of petrol burners be installed on the approach to Runway 5. The distance between them was calculated so that at the critical height of 200ft on the approach an aircraft crew should be able to pick out the high-density approach lighting and land safely.

On 7 February 1952, the new Queen, HM Queen Elizabeth II, arrived at London Airport in a Boac Argonaut from Entebbe at 4.19p.m., and disembarked to take her first steps on British soil as monarch, following the death of her father while she was in Africa. The spot where she disembarked is now part of the Heathrow Renaissance Hotel, and is marked by a plaque in the Brasserie Restaurant. A new point-to-point World Class speed record was set on 18 February when a Canberra jet bomber flew from London Airport to Castel Benito in Libya in 2 hours, 44 minutes at an average speed of 538mph. Transatlantic air travel for the masses came a step nearer on 1 May 1952 when the first Tourist Class services between Europe and North America were inaugurated by Pan American Airways and BOAC. Pan American used Douglas DC-6Bs on their 'Rainbow' service between London and New York, and BOAC used Constellations on their 'Mayflower' service to New York and their 'Beaver' service to Canada. On the following day BOAC inaugurated the world's first regular passenger service by jet airliner. Comet 1 G-ALYP left London Airport with thirty-six passengers aboard and flew to Johannesburg via Rome, Beirut, Khartoum, Entebbe and Livingstone in 23 hours, 34 minutes. The fare was £175 one-way or £315 return, and further Comet routes to Colombo and Tokyo were introduced in August 1952 and April 1953. BEA's 'Elizabethan' class Airspeed Ambassadors finally entered full-time service on the Paris route on 27 March 1952, and from 16 June they were used to revive the pre-war 'Silver Wing' luxury service to Paris formerly operated by Imperial Airways out of Croydon. The lunchtime flight BE333 left London at 1.00p.m. each day on a schedule that was deliberately set at a leisurely pace of 1 hour, 30 minutes' duration to allow the passengers to savour a four-course lunch of potted Morecambe shrimps, roast Norfolk turkey, Cape pears in port, and cheese and biscuits. The fare of £15 19s 0d return also included complimentary champagne and cigarettes, and the cabin was laid out in a spacious forty-seat configuration. The Silver Wing service was handled with military precision by the BEA ground staff. All baggage was to be loaded by 12.40p.m., and the passengers were boarded 10 minutes later. As the engines were started, there were three traffic officers in attendance, an engineer to report 'chocks away', an apron observer to record the departure time, and the senior traffic officer to salute the aircraft as it began to taxi. Travellers to Paris with less money to spare could still travel for £9 15s 0d return on a forty-seven-seat Night Tourist service.

Military aircraft still paid occasional visits to the airport. On 10 July 1952, test pilot David Morgan took off in a Supermarine Swift jet fighter for Brussels (Melsbroek) to participate in a NATO-sponsored flying display. He completed the 200.38-mile journey in a record-breaking 18 minutes, 3.3 seconds at an average speed of 665.9mph. Another military jet to pay a visit that year was a de Havilland Vampire flown by 'Moose' Davies. He was participating in Exercise Ardent, flying from a base in Northern Germany to carry out a simulated attack on London when he suffered a barostat failure which closed his engine down to idle thrust. After making an emergency descent through cloud he saw a large airfield with many aircraft on it which he took to be a US air base. Although the runway in use at the time was 10R he accomplished a safe landing on Runway 23L. After repairs the Vampire departed for Bovingdon on 14 October. BOAC continued to expand its network of tourist-class services on 17 November by offering savings of up to 28 per cent on flights to the Sudan, Uganda and Kenya operated by Handley Page Hermes aircraft. BEA carried out its first Royal flight on 26 November when Elizabethan G-AMAB carried HRH the Duke of Edinburgh to Malta. The same aircraft returned the Duke to London on 2 December, calling at Rome en route to collect HRH the Duchess of Kent.

On 10 December 1952, Mr A.T. Lennox-Boyd, the Minister for Civil Aviation, announced in the House of Commons that London Airport was not to be extended to the north of the Bath Road after all. He said that a careful analysis of the practical experiments recently concluded by his department had shown that the additional amount of traffic that could be accepted by extending the airport to the north of the Bath Road would not justify the expenditure and disturbance which would be incurred. The decision would save some £10 million of capital investment and the homes of some 650 families. It was thought that in its present form with six runways the airport should eventually be capable of handling about ninety aircraft each hour, although the present location of the temporary control tower and passenger terminals was preventing the full use of Runways 7 and 4. (The Government Ministry responsible for civil aviation underwent several changes of name during the late 1940s and the 1950s. On the resumption of civil flying after the war it was called the Ministry of Civil Aviation. In October 1953, the title was changed to the Ministry of Transport and Civil Aviation, but on 14 October 1959 it resumed its former title. On 15 October 1970, all transport responsibilities were subsumed by the Department of the Environment.) During 1952 the number of passengers totalled around 861,000 and the volume of freight handled was in the region of 15,300 short tons, an increase of 6 per cent on 1951. Each day there were around 100 aircraft movements.

On 18 April 1953, BEA inaugurated the world's first sustained passenger service by turbo-prop airliner when Vickers Viscount G-AMNY flew London-Rome-Athens-Nicosia, the last leg being operated on charter to Cyprus Airways. At that time, BEA's Apron Control Office was one of a row of pre-fabricated buildings on the north side apron. It was entered through a door marked 'SABENA', and offered its occupants a precarious view of the airport through a screen of mobile aircraft steps and the occasional parked baggage lorry. The officer in charge was Gerald Wynne, and other officials included Duty Officer Ben Wellman, Interline Officer Peter Mantle and Senior Traffic Officers E.C.Kent and Keith Hayward. BEA carried out all the apron handling for Air France, Iberia, SABENA, SAS and Swissair. The apron observers were equipped with 'walkie-talkie' two-way radios strapped to their backs and used bicycles to get around the tarmac. Motor scooters had been tried out but had proved too delicate. The introduction of cheap fare services was still gaining momentum. On 3 April 1953, Central African Airways began a weekly 'Zambesi' Colonial Coach service from Salisbury in Rhodesia to London using Vickers Vikings, the first such schedule being operated by VP-YHJ 'RMA Sabi'. That year, Pan American were advertising their 'Rainbow' tourist-class services from London into Europe. Passengers could fly on eighty-two-seat Douglas DC-6Bs from London to Frankfurt for £26 19s 0d return, or to Brussels or Amsterdam for £14 17s 0d return. SABENA were offering flights from London to Nice via Brussels for £27 10s 0d return. Travel from London to Brussels was by Convair 240, with onward transportation to Nice by their brand new DC-6Bs.

BOAC Comet services continued to slash travel times worldwide. Comet crew members reported to Dormy House, near Sunningdale, and if the service was scheduled to depart between midnight and 9.00a.m., they were normally accommodated there during their rest period before the flight. BOAC coaches brought the passengers to the airport from Airways Terminal at Victoria, arriving 45 minutes before scheduled flight departure. They were met by a Passenger Handling receptionist and escorted to the ticket counter, then through Customs and Immigration and on to the departure lounge. The deadline for passengers arriving by private car was 30 minutes before departure. A list of passenger names, weights and destinations was transferred by Lamson vacuum tube from the ticket counter to the first floor, where Service Control staff made final amendments to the passenger manifest. On 2 May 1953, on the first anniversary of Comet operations, G-ALYV broke up during a storm and crashed near Calcutta. Comet operations continued normally however, and on 30 June, HRH the Queen

Mother and HRH Princess Margaret departed London at 1.15p.m. on board Comet G-ALYW for Salisbury in Rhodesia for the Rhodes Centenary celebrations. During June 1953 William McMillan RA was continuing to work on a memorial to the pioneer transatlantic aviators, Alcock and Brown. This was to be sited initially overlooking the north side apron, but by September 1953, the intention was for it to be moved to the Central Area and placed opposite the entrance to the Central Area Administration Building and facing west, once that building had been completed. A public appeal for funds for its construction had been launched in September 1952, and by June 1953 over £3,500 of its total cost of £5,000 had been subscribed. During that month, the spectators' enclosure was temporarily relocated to an area on the temporarily closed runway 28R. Among the attractions provided were a small funfair and a miniature train ride.

During 1953 around 527,000 spectators visited the airport and there was much for them to see. 2 June 1953 was Coronation Day, and newsreel film of the ceremony was despatched around the world by air. The RAF organised Operation Pony Express to fly film to Canada on that day. Two Bristol Sycamore helicopters carried batches of film from a cricket ground alongside Alexandra Palace to London Airport in around 9 minutes. Three Canberra jet bombers, plus one in reserve, were waiting to depart for Goose Bay, where the film was transferred to CF-100 jets of the Royal Canadian Air Force for onward transportation to Montreal. The American television companies hired commercial airliners as 'flying newsrooms' complete with cine editing equipment. NBC chartered a DC-6B from Pan American Airways to fly non-stop from London to Boston, while CBS hired a BOAC Stratocruiser which also flew to Boston via Gander. One day during the autumn KLM showed off its new Super Constellation equipment by replacing the scheduled Convair 240 on the Amsterdam-London service with L-1049C Super Constellation PH-FFS *Proton*. During its stopover in London it gave a 30-minute demonstration flight to airline officials, journalists and travel agents.

On 19 September, the Battle of Britain was commemorated with a static display of military aircraft which included an RAF Meteor, Vampire, Canberra and Varsity and a Royal Canadian Air Force F-86 Sabre. Between 8 and 10 October 1953, London Airport was the starting point for the London-Christchurch (NZ) Air Race. The race was divided into a Speed Section and a Transport Handicap Section. Each section offered prizes of £10,000 for the winner and £3,000 for the runner-up, and there was also a gold cup for the winner of the Speed Section. The RAF and Royal Australian Air Force each entered Canberra jet bombers comprising two Canberra PR3s, a PR7 and two Australian-built B.20s, but the first aircraft away was a KLM DC-6A at 4.30p.m., followed by a Royal New Zealand Air Force Hastings transport and the prototype Viscount Viscount 700, which had been leased from Vickers by BEA. All of the competitors were flagged away by their Prince Henry, Duke of Gloucester, and after the transport aircraft had gone the Canberras departed at 5-minute intervals. For the period of the race preparations and start a new

An Island Air Services Rapide sets off on another sightseeing flight in the 1950s. (John Carter)

A view of the north side spectators' enclosure in the 1950s, showing the terminal building and two SAS DC-4s. (John Carter)

Top: An aerial view of the north side apron and buildings, with the Bath Road on the left of the photo. (Vic Attwood)

Middle: A BOAC DC-7C in the airline's 'white-top' livery. (John Hamlin)

Left: British United Britannia freighter G-ANCD, used on the Africargo service. (Vic Attwood)

temporary public enclosure was opened in the Central Area near to the former Fairey hangar. The tunnel into the Central Area was opened to the public for the first time on 5 October, and the race aircraft were lined up on display, with spectators being permitted to peer into the Canberra crew compartments. An RAF Canberra PR3 won the Speed Section and the Transport Handicap Section was won by the KLM DC-6A, which had carried a full complement of fare-paying emigrant passengers.

In 1953 the new £20,000 RSPCA animal hostel at the airport was opened and during that year it handled 323,054 animals. The majority of these were in transit through London. During 1954 BOAC operated a once-weekly York freighter service to Singapore with stops at Tripoli, Cairo, Bahrein, Karachi, Delhi, Calcutta and Bangkok. Mainly general cargo was carried on the outward journey, but on the return leg the bulk of the cargo was animals uplifted from Bangkok, Calcutta, Delhi and Karachi. Monkeys,

The very idea of the Royal Aeronautical Society holding a garden party between the runways at Heathrow would be pure fantasy for most of us - This is the list of arrivals and departures from noon onwards which guests could expect to see at such an event in 1954! Wonderful............

SCHEDULED SERVICES FOR SUNDAY 13th JUNE 1954

ARRIVALS				DEPARTURES			
Time: p.m.	Operator	Aircraft	From	Time: p.m.	Operator	Aircraft	To
12.05	B.O.A.C.	Constellation	New York/Prestwick	12 noon	B.E.A.	Elizabethan	Paris
12.10	B.O.A.C.	Argonaut	Bahrein/Düsseldorf	12 noon	P.A.A.	Stratocruiser	Frankfurt
12.25	T.W.A.	Constellation	New York	12.20	Air France	DC-3	Dinard
12.45	B.E.A.	Viscount	Copenhagen	12.25	B.E.A.	Viscount	Frankfurt
12.45	Air France	Viscount	Paris	12.30	Air France	DC-4	Paris
1.00	S.A.S.	DC-6	Oslo/Stavanger	12.40	Sabena	Convair	Brussels
1.15	S.A.S.	DC-6	Stockholm/Copenhagen	12.50	B.E.A.	Elizabethan	Amsterdam
1.30	B.O.A.C.	Argonaut	Nairobi/Rome	1.00	B.E.A.	Elizabethan	Paris
1.50	B.E.A.	Elizabethan	Paris	1.00	K.L.M.	Convair	Amsterdam
1.55	B.E.A.	Viscount	Stockholm/Oslo	1.10	T.W.A.	Constellation	Frankfurt
1.55	B.O.A.C.	Argonaut	Nairobi/Rome	1.30	Air France	Viscount	Paris
2.15	B.O.A.C.	Constellation	New York/Prestwick	1.35	B.E.A.	Viscount	Palma
2.25	Air France	DC-4	Paris	2.00	B.E.A.	Elizabethan	Paris
2.50	B.E.A.	Elizabethan	Paris	2.05	B.E.A.	Viscount	Oslo/Stockholm
3.00	B.O.A.C.	York (freighter)	Singapore/Castel Benito	2.45	B.O.A.C.	Argonaut	Rome/Accra
3.50	S.A.A.	Constellation	Johannesburg/Rome	2.55	B.E.A.	Elizabethan	Amsterdam
3.50	B.E.A.	Elizabethan	Paris	3.15	Air France	DC-4	Paris
4.20	Alitalia	Convair	Milan	3.25	B.E.A.	Viscount	Copenhagen
4.20	Sabena	Convair	Brussels	3.35	S.A.S.	DC-6	Gothenburg/Stockholm
4.20	B.O.A.C.	Argonaut	Colombo/Rome	4.00	B.E.A.	Elizabethan	Paris
4.25	Swissair	Convair	Geneva	4.20	S.A.S.	DC-6	Copenhagen/Stockholm
4.35	Air France	DC-4	Paris	5.00	B.E.A.	Elizabethan	Paris
4.35	B.E.A.	Viscount	Geneva	5.10	Sabena	Convair	Brussels
4.35	B.E.A.	Elizabethan	Hamburg	5.25	Alitalia	Convair	Milan/Rome
4.50	B.E.A.	Elizabethan	Paris	5.30	Air France	DC-4	Paris
4.55	K.L.M.	Convair	Amsterdam	5.40	B.E.A.	Elizabethan	Düsseldorf/Berlin
5.00	Swissair	DC-6B	Zürich	5.45	Swissair	DC-6B	Zürich
5.15	B.E.A.	Elizabethan	Amsterdam	6.15	B.E.A.	Elizabethan	Amsterdam
5.30	B.E.A.	Viscount	Zürich	7.00	P.A.A.	Stratocruiser	New York
5.50	B.E.A.	Elizabethan	Paris	7.00	K.L.M.	Convair	Amsterdam
6.00	B.E.A.	Viscount	Frankfurt	7.00	B.E.A.	Elizabethan	Paris
6.05	Swissair	Convair	Zürich/Basle	7.00	B.O.A.C.	Argonaut	Tokyo
6.10	Swissair	DC-3	Berne	7.05	B.E.A.	Viscount	Glasgow
6.15	B.E.A.	Viscount	Istanbul	7.20	B.E.A.	Viscount	Belfast
6.15	B.E.A.	Elizabethan	Nice	7.30	P.A.A.	DC-6	New York
6.25	P.A.A.	DC-6	Frankfurt	7.50	B.E.A.	Elizabethan	Brussels
6.30	B.E.A.	Viscount	Madrid	7.55	B.E.A.	Viscount	Manchester
6.30	B.E.A.	Elizabethan	Cologne/Brussels	8.03	B.O.A.C.	Stratocruiser	New York
6.45	B.E.A.	Viscount	Barcelona	8.00	Air France	DC-4	Paris
6.55	B.E.A.	Elizabethan	Amsterdam	8.15	B.E.A.	Viscount	Birmingham
7.05	Air France	DC-4	Paris				
7.05	Qantas	Constellation	Sydney/Frankfurt				
7.50	Qantas	Constellation	Sydney/Frankfurt				
7.50	B.E.A.	Elizabethan	Paris				
8.00	K.L.M.	Convair	Amsterdam				
8.05	T.W.A.	Constellation	Frankfurt				
8.10	Air France	DC-3	Nice/Marseilles				
8.20	B.E.A.	Viscount	Athens/Rome				
8.25	B.E.A.	Elizabethan	Rome/Nice				
8.25	B.E.A.	Viscount	Vienna/Zürich				
8.25	Air France	DC-4	Paris				
8.50	B.E.A.	Elizabethan	Paris				
8.55	Air India	Constellation	Calcutta/Paris				

NOTES:

The details were correct at the time of going to press and are liable to alteration. There will also be unscheduled services.

If, as is often the case, there is a westerly wind, landings will be on No. 5 runway, near the Garden Party area and just to the south of it, and take-offs will be from No. 1 runway near the Bath Road and about ¼-mile to the north.

An extract from the programme for the Royal Aeronautical Society Garden Party of 13 June 1954, showing the scheduled airliner movements to be expected that day. (Via Keith Hayward, British Airways Archives)

birds and fish were the most common loads and sometimes there were as many as 5,000 monkeys on a single flight, most of them bound for onward transportation to zoos and research laboratories in the USA. During one month in 1954 the RSPCA hostel handled 37,140 animals including 30,160 finches and 3,289 monkeys.

On 1 November 1953 Trans-Canada Air Lines opened a new route to Toronto via Prestwick using Canadair North Stars, and on 23-24 November BOAC carried HM the Queen and HRH the Duke of Edinburgh to Bermuda via Gander aboard Stratocruiser G-AKGK *RMA Canopus* under the command of Captain A. C. Lorraine. The flight was the start of their Commonwealth Tour and was the first transatlantic crossing by air by a reigning British monarch. On 2 December Air France inaugurated regular Viscount services between Paris and London. The new turbo-props were first allocated to the airline's 'Epicurean' service, in competition with BEA's Silver Wing flights. During 1953 the airport handled more than one million passengers for the first time in its history and around 527,000 people paid their *6d* to pass through the turnstiles of the public enclosure.

1954 began with a disaster; on 10 January, BOAC Comet G-ALYP was on a service from the Far East to London when it broke up in mid-air near Elba. All the Comets were grounded, but returned to service on 23 March. Then, on 8 April, Comet G-ALYY disintegrated in mid-flight near Naples and the Comet fleet was again grounded, this time permanently. The resulting aircraft shortage led to the suspension of all BOAC services to South America, and in July the Hermes fleet which had been retired in October 1953 had to be temporarily returned to service on the routes to East Africa. During 1954 the north side apron occupied an area which later became the site of the Heathrow Penta Hotel. To ease congestion the eastern half of Runway 28R was taken out of service and used for overflow parking of aircraft. Departing aircraft still used the remaining western end of the runway, while arrivals landed on Runway 28L. By April 1954 London Airport was

Hunting Clan Avro York G-ANGF. (Vic Attwood)

one of only six civil airports in the UK equipped with GCA radar. The number of GCA landings since 1947 had passed the 38,000 mark, and during December 1954 a record 1467 full GCA landings were accomplished, around 85 per cent of the total number of landings that month. The airport was the only British airport with two complete GCA caravans, to enable changes in runway direction to be handled with the minimum of delay, and to provide a back-up facility in the event of one becoming unserviceable. On 13 June 1954, the Royal Aeronautical Society held its Garden Party at the airport on a cold and wet Sunday afternoon. On show and available for internal inspection were a BEA Viscount and Ambassador, a BOAC Stratocruiser, a Trans-Canada Airlines L-1049C Super Constellation, and a BEA Bristol 171 helicopter. Conducted bus tours of the airport installations were on offer, and holders of lucky programme numbers were taken up for local sightseeing flights in a BEA Viscount in between the normal scheduled airline movements. Two days later BEA used its Bristol 171 helicopter G-AMWH to inaugurate helicopter services between London Airport and Southampton via Northolt. The first public service took place on the following day, when three passengers were carried from London to Southampton at a fare of £1 10s 0d.

Also on 15 June, the statue of Alcock and Brown was unveiled on the north side apron by Mr Lennox-Boyd, the Minister for Civil Aviation, accompanied by Lord Brabazon of Tara, the President of the Royal Aero Club. The ceremony marked the 35th anniversary of the pioneer flyers' transatlantic flight, and before the unveiling Lord Brabazon gave a speech which painted a picture of flying as it was in 1919. A total of £3,845 had

The battered hulk of BEA Viscount 701 G-AMOK in the Central Area after its accident on 16 January 1955. (Michael Wall)

SABENA Convair 340 OO-AWR awaits its passengers in the Central Area on 7 July 1954. (SABENA)

been raised towards the £5,000 needed, with contributions coming from both sides of the Atlantic. Between 400 and 500 Americans including Colonel Lindbergh had made donations. On 3 October 1954 Hunting-Clan Air Transport transferred its Newcastle-London route from Northolt to London Airport, and on 30 October Northolt was closed to scheduled airline services. BEA's last movement out of Northolt was a positioning flight to London Airport by Viking G-AIVI. On board for the occasion were senior representatives from BEA, Vickers-Armstrong, the Ministry of Civil Aviation, Aer Lingus, and the Engine Division of the Bristol Aeroplane Company. The Viking took off at 8.12p.m. and overflew Chatham, Sevenoaks and Gatwick before finally touching down at London Airport at 8.53p.m.

On 29 November 1954, BEA Ambassador G-ALZR lost both nosewheels shortly after taking off for Amsterdam with forty passengers on board. After flying around for two hours to burn off fuel and having all the baggage in the interior front compartment moved to the rear toilet area, Captain James Cooke landed safely on Runway 10R on the mainwheels and the stub of the nosewheel leg and was later awarded the Queens Commendation for Valuable Service in the Air. BEA suffered another accident on

SABENA Convair 340 OO-AWR in a rather deserted Central Area on 6 July 1954. (SABENA)

16 January 1955. Viscount 701 G-AMOK was scheduled to operate flight BE130 to Istanbul via Rome and Athens, and taxied out in conditions of poor visibility. The flight was cleared to taxi along Runway 1 (now Runway 27R) to the holding point for Runway Six (now Runway 15R), but due to the visibility problems the crew accidentally turned onto the disued Runway 3 and began their take-off run. This runway had been out of service since 1949 and was being used for the storage of construction equipment. The Viscount ran into a collection of contractors' equipment and stores and ploughed through a steel barrier, some huts and a pile of cast iron, shedding both port engines and rupturing the fuel tanks. However, there was no fire, and only the captain and one passenger were injured. In February 1955 the airport had its first visit from an Ilyushin 14 aircraft, a Soviet Air Force VIP example bringing Mr Gromyko from Moscow via Berlin for a Five-Power Conference. On the last leg of its journey, the aircraft carried two RAF navigators to assist the Russian crew with Western air traffic control procedures. This was necessary as the Russian crew spoke no English, and the RAF members also had to act as translators during radio exchanges with the GCA controllers on the ground. The delay caused by this procedure resulted in two overshoots and the situation was only resolved when a Russian Air Attach went into the control tower to assist. All-cargo services to Idlewild Airport in New York, with refuelling stops at Keflavik and Gander, were inaugurated by the British independent airline Airwork on 1 March 1955. Leased Transocean Airways DC-4s were used initially, but Airwork then ordered new DC-6As for the service. The airline also opened feeder services with cargo Vikings from Aden, Frankfurt and Zurich to London, but the transatlantic service was suspended after little over nine months of operation and the Viking services ceased on 8 March 1956.

On 15 April 1955, Lufthansa Convair 340 D-ACAD made the first post-war landing in the UK by a German civil-registered aircraft, on a proving flight from Hamburg to London prior to the commencement of Lufthansa schedule services in May.

6

THE CENTRAL AREA

As early as 1952, the MCA was showing reluctance to sanction the construction of any further buildings on the already inadequate north side area because of the planned transfer of all passenger handling and air traffic control facilities to the 54-acre Central Area site. This was to be the location of two main passenger terminals, one for short-haul flights and the other for intercontinental services. The foundations had already been laid for a new control tower and work had started on a 2,400ft road tunnel under No.1 Runway to link the Central Area with the Bath Road. The first stage of the central Area complex came into operation on 17 April 1955 when the new control tower became operational and around two-thirds of what was initially named the South-East Face Passenger Handling Building was opened for domestic and European services, the first schedule being operated to Amsterdam by BEA Viscount 701 G-AMOA. The aircraft parking area was in the shape of a diamond, with spaces for thirty-four aircraft on the north-east and south-east faces, although initially only the south-east face was in use. The parking areas were divided by one taxiway and enclosed by a second, with the outer stands being accessed by vehicles via a subway emerging on the outer perimeter of the apron. Passengers for aircraft using these outer stands had to be bussed to and from the terminal. A waiting area for cars staying longer than 20 minutes was situated alongside the passenger buildings, and a long-stay car park was laid out on a triangular site near the exit from the tunnel. Spectators' cars had to turn left out of the tunnel and follow road signs leading to car parks with a capacity of some 1,500 vehicles. The new nine-storey control tower was 127ft high and was topped by a penthouse housing the aerodrome control staff. In the approach control room two radar controllers guided in aircraft from the Epsom and Watford stacks using the twin-stack feed system. When the

Sabena Convair 240 OO-AWP in the Central Area on 10 May 1955. In the background, work goes on to complete the terminal complex. (SABENA)

The control tower in the Central Area on 10 May 1955, shortly after it became operational. (SABENA)

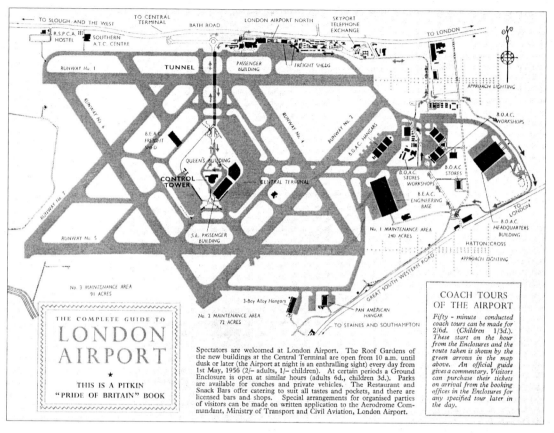

An extract from a mid-'50s guidebook to London Airport, including details of the spectators' facilities, and the coach tours of the airport. (Pitkin Pictorials Ltd via Author)

aircraft were six or seven miles from the airport, they were handed over (if necessary) to the GCA talkdown controller. He was initially still based in a GCA caravan near the runway but was later to move into the tower's approach control room. Using full talk-down a landing rate of three aircraft each minute could be achieved. With the opening of the control tower the London Air Traffic Control Centre was transferred across from Uxbridge, where it had been linked to the airport by five miles of telephone wires.

On 16 May 1955, the West German state airline Lufthansa resumed flying to London its first post-war services. Convair 340 D-ACOH operated from Munich via Frankfurt, while its sister ship D-ACIG flew Hamburg-Dusseldorf-London. At that time a number of BEA captains were on secondment to Lufthansa, flying in command while sufficient numbers of Lufthansa captains were being trained. BOAC inaugurated its first tourist-class Stratocruiser service to New York via Manchester, but on 22 June the airline lost the smallest member of its fleet. De Havilland Dove G-ALTM was on a photographic

Lufthansa's post-war inaugural service to London. Convair 340 D-ACOH in the Central Area on 16 May 1955. Sharing the apron are BEA Dakota and Ambassador aircraft, and behind them the former Fairey hangar. (Lufthansa)

A Lufthansa Convair 340 taxies past another example in the Central Area. (Via Author)

Top: Westpoint Aviation Dakota G-ALYF, used on services to the West Country. (Frank Hudson)

Middle: European Asiatic DC-4 N9702F, an unusual visitor to the Central Area. (Frank Hudson)

Bottom: European Asiatic DC-4 N9702F, an unusual visitor to the Central Area. (Frank Hudson)

Left: Aeroflot TU-104 CCCP-L5400 makes the first visit of the type on 22 March 1958. (Frank Hudson)

Below: Transair Viscount G-AOXU in the Central Area in the late 1950s. (Frank Hudson)

Below: Air France Viscount 708 F-BGNT in front of the Central Area terminal complex in the mid-1950s. (Air France)

sortie when its starboard engine lost power. By mistake the healthy port engine was then shut down, and while the aircraft was on approach to London Airport, the ailing starboard engine failed completely. The Dove crashed, but the pilots and two BOAC photographers on board escaped with minor injuries. In July 1955 BEA introduced scheduled helicopter services from the Central Area to the South Bank Heliport at Waterloo in London. Westland WS-55s were used, flying five round-trips each day on a routeing that took them from the airport to overhead Kew Bridge, then along the line of the Thames to the South Bank. The service ended on 31 May 1956, by which time 3,822 revenue passengers had been carried. The opening of the Central Area complex relieved the north side terminal of some 60 per cent of its passengers, but it continued in use for long-haul services. The facilities there remained rather basic, and in the mid-1950s there was no designated car park for aircrew. Those crew members fortunate enough to own a car had to park them on the side of the road or on a patch of waste ground. It was to be another six years before long-haul operations switched to the Central Area, and in the meantime more new services began life on the north side. On 23 July 1955 Hunting-Clan Air Transport inaugurated its freight-only 'Africargo' service to Africa. The flights actually originated at Manchester and called in at London en route to Salisbury via Malta, Khartoum, Entebbe and Nairobi. Initially Avro Yorks were used on a weekly basis, but by the end of September the frequency had been doubled, and in August 1958 brand new Douglas DC-6Cs arrived to replace the Yorks. Later, Hunting-Clan was to merge with Airwork to form British United Airways, and from 1966 converted Bristol Britannia turbo-props took over on the service.

On 16 December 1955 the Central Area terminal buildings and control tower were officially inaugurated by HM the Queen. She wore a coat of Air Force Blue, with a grey hat and a diamond lapel brooch in the shape of the BOAC 'speedbird' logo, and was greeted by a guard of honour made up of aircrew members from British and commonwealth airlines headed by BOAC captain J.C. Percy. Sarah Boyd-Carpenter, the daughter of the Minister of Transport, presented an arrangement of flowers from all over the world that had been flown into the airport by four commonwealth airlines. In her speech the Queen said: 'For centuries London has been a port from which vessels have set out for the farthest corners of the earth. It has been, and is, a great centre of commerce. In the new era of flight which has transformed our world in less than half a century, London has acquired a new importance.' At the end of her speech Her Majesty disclosed the new name of the Eastern Apex Building when she unveiled a plaque naming it the Queen's Building. This building on the London-facing side of the terminal building housed airline flight-planning and briefing rooms, operations and meteorological offices, and an aircrew customs hall as well as visitor facilities which included a post office, 160-seat news cinema, buffet and grill room. The roof was designed as a series of gardens, including a circular ornamental pool with fountain.

Swissair DC-6B HB-IBI in the Central Area. The Pan American and Hunting-Clan hangars are in the far background. (Air-Britain)

SAS DC-6B OY-KLY in the Central Area. (Air-Britain)

On its airside edge were viewing terraces on five levels, and the roof of the Queen's Building was connected to the roof gardens on top of the terminal building by an 80ft footbridge. By the spring of 1956 the spectator facilities had become London's most visited tourist attraction, with the revenue from the admission charges (1s for adults and 6d for children) exceeding that of the Tower of London and Windsor Castle. Day trippers came by coach from all over England and Wales and a bus ride through the tunnel could be enjoyed for 2d. BOAC employees were encouraged to bring their families and friends on Sundays for a free guided tour of the airport which ended with tea in BOAC's new headquarters building (known by staff as the 'Kremlin') Providing a commentary on the aircraft movements from his office in the control tower was Stan Little, who had completed two seasons as commentator at Northolt before taking up his post at London Airport. He was later to transfer his base to a cubicle on the roof of the Queen's Building, and to be joined by former WRAF Flying Officer Flo Kingdon. She usually alternated her shifts with Stan Little, but on busy weekends they often doubled up. After nine years in the post, she later became a public-relations officer at the airport and part of the Queen's Building management team. The new passenger terminal was a modernistic red-brick and glass structure and featured a series of channels for departing and arriving passengers. Departing passengers would disembark from the bus from the town terminal in front of one of ten numbered bays, each of which had been pre-allocated to a particular flight. Passengers using Channel 4, for example, would enter the lower hall and ascend by dedicated escalator to the main concourse that ran the full length of the first floor. Meanwhile, their luggage was unloaded from the coach and transported by moving belt to the Channel 4 customs bay on the floor above. After examination it continued on the belt to the apron loading bays. Passengers passed through Customs and then arrived at the south-east face of the building which comprised a series of waiting rooms, each one allocated to a particular passenger channel. All of these channels were quickly reversible to enable them to handle incoming flights as well. Overlooking the apron was a restaurant and an outdoor 'waving base' for the friends of passengers. Cantilevered out from the restaurant roof was a glazed cubicle from where the marshalling supervisor controlled aircraft movements on the apron.

On 27 January 1956 HM the Queen and HRH the Duke of Edinburgh set off from the airport in a BOAC Argonaut at the start of their Royal Tour of Nigeria. The first visit to the UK of a Soviet-built jet airliner took place on 22 March 1956 when Aeroflot Tupolev TU-104 CCCP-L5400 arrived at London from Moscow. It was carrying Colonel Ivan Serov, Russia's top security chief for military intelligence, who was visiting to make sure that the arrangements were satisfactory for the official visit later that month of Communist Party First Secretary Nikita Kruschev and Soviet Premier Nikolai Bulganin. The TU-104 made one pass over the airport at around 2,000ft before landing on Runway 15R. On 25 April, no less than three TU-104s (CCCP-L5400,

Above: Alitalia DC-7C I-DUVI in the Central Area. Behind it is the former Fairey hangar, now sporting a BOAC advertising hoarding. (Air-Britain)

Left: Swissair Convair 240 HB-IRZ still wears Swiss Air Lines titles, although the van in the foreground has been repainted in the new livery. (Air-Britain)

Aeroflot TU-104 CCCP-L5400 during the first visit of the new Soviet jetliner on 22 March 1956. (Air-Britain)

L5412 and L5413) arrived from Moscow on proving flights in connection with the eventual introduction of the type on scheduled services into London. The north side complex was still in use and still hosting new services. On 10 April, Seaboard and Western Airlines opened New York-Shannon-London scheduled all-cargo services with L-1049H Super Constellations, and on 21 April South African Airways introduced Douglas DC-7Bs onto their 'Springbok' service from Johannesburg. Around 1956/7 a small café on the north side of the A4 main road and opposite Block 7 on the north side apron was in use, and featured a jukebox which played records when 3d was inserted into the slot. Around 1958 a large Nissen hut close to the original control tower became the new Green Dragon Café and was patronised by airport workers and aircraft spotters until at least 1965.

On 18 June 1956, HM the Queen took her first flight in a Viscount when she flew from Stockholm to London with their Royal Highnesses Princess Margaret and the Duke and Duchess of Gloucester aboard BEA example G-ANHC. On 16 September, Battle of Britain Day was once again commemorated at the airport with a static display of RAF aircraft lined up on the old spectators' area above the tunnel entrance. The exhibits comprised a Canberra PR3, a Hastings C2, a Meteor NF14, a Venom NF3 and a Hunter F6. Another RAF aircraft was expected to arrive on 1 October when Vulcan B.1 XA897, the first RAF example, was due to land at the conclusion of its tour to Australia and New Zealand. A ground-controlled approach was made to runway 10L, but the Vulcan struck the ground about 2,000ft short of the runway and bounced back into the air before finally crashing onto the runway. The pilot and Air Marshall Broadhurst, who was occupying the co-pilot's seat, ejected and survived, but the other four occupants including a civilian contractor perished. Early in 1957 BOAC introduced two new types into service, with Douglas DC-7Cs taking over the London-New York 'Monarch' service on 6 January, and Britannia 102 G-ANBI inaugurating the airline's first turbo-prop services on 1 February with a three-times-weekly schedule to Johannesburg. A glimpse of what might have been occurred on 1 June when the Fairey Rotodyne vertical take-off convertiplane flew from London Airport to Brussels and back and then to Paris for the Paris Air Show. It made another visit to the airport in June 1958, and BEA had plans to use the Rotodyne on services to Paris city centre, but these never came to fruition and the aircraft was eventually broken up. BOAC suffered a mishap on 11 August 1957. Constellation G-ANNT was approaching London from Frankfurt with seventeen occupants on the last leg of a service from Singapore when it suffered a hydraulics failure which prevented the crew from lowering the main undercarriage. After circling for about three hours to burn off fuel and making repeated approaches to Runway 28L they made an emergency landing on Runway 23L as the light was fading. This runway was chosen so as to avoid blocking the main runway. The Constellation came to rest just before the intersection with Runway 28L with no injuries to anyone aboard.

Seaboard and Western Super Constellation freighter N6503C taxies in to the north side apron. (Air-Britain)

BOAC Constellation G-ANNT after landing with an undercarriage problem on 11 August 1957. (Eric Loseby)

One of Shell's executive Airspeed Ambassadors in the Central Area in 1965. (Author)

An unusual visitor to the airport. Air Safaris Hermes G-ALDL is marshalled onto its stand in the Central Area. (Air-Britain)

In August 1957 the Millbourn Report on London Airport was published. Amongst its principal recommendations were:

That the airport be developed by 1970 to handle up to eighty movements each hour during peak times, with total annual traffic of 211,000 aircraft movements and 12.75 million passengers.

That terminal facilities for all services, including cargo, should be provided in the Central Area. The expansion of the Central Area should be achieved by withdrawing No.4 runway from use and using it to provide an additional 52 acres. If more aircraft stands were eventually needed, No.6 runway should be withdrawn from use to provide an extra 40 acres.

That a long-haul terminal should be constructed in the Central Area as quickly as possible, and that a second terminal to handle the growth in short haul traffic should be constructed when required.

That piers from the passenger buildings onto the apron should be built, to eliminate the need for bus transfers.

That a new cargo building should be built in the Central Area, to the left of the tunnel entrance.

That schemes for encouraging motorists to leave their cars outside of the Central Area should be given close consideration.

That a decision on the advisability of linking the airport with the centre of London (i.e. Victoria) by rail should be taken before the detailed planning of the road system within the Central Area is completed.

The Report rejected the suggestion of transferring BEA's domestic services to the North terminal and the development of a new long-haul terminal in the south-west No.3 maintenance area.

In September 1957 the two US operators commenced services to the west coast of America via the Polar Route. Pan American inaugurated DC-7C services from London to Seattle and San Francisco via Frobisher Bay on Baffin Island on 11 September, and by 30 September TWA began flying L-1649A Starliners over the Pole from Los Angeles,

Swissair Convair 440 HB-IMB in the Central Area in the late 1950s. (Frank Hudson)

followed by San Francisco-London polar services from 2 October. BOAC stepped up the competition on 19 December when it introduced the first transatlantic turbo-prop services with Britannia 312s operating from London to New York. BOAC's Far East cargo services were still using venerable Avro Yorks, operated on their behalf between London and Singapore by the independent airline Skyways. During 1957, the airport handled around 11,600 aircraft movements, 3.5 million passengers and approximately 60,000 tons of freight. Forty-two airlines from thirty-two countries operated scheduled services through the airport and around 25,000 people were employed there.

On 21 September 1958 London Airport once again hosted a static display of RAF aircraft to commemorate Battle of Britain Day. This time the types on display comprised a Comet 2, a Vulcan B.1, a Beverley C.1, a Javelin FAW.7, a Hunter F.6, and a Victor B.1. Earlier in the month, the Boeing 707 visited for the first time when Pan American's example N709PA *Clipper America* arrived for noise tests. Another visit was made for the same purpose on 3 October, but the type was not destined to provide the first scheduled transatlantic jet services. On 30 September, BOAC's first two Comet 4s were handed over at London Airport and on 2 October G-APDB departed for New York via Gander on a 'pre-inaugural proving flight'. On board were the Managing Directors of BOAC and de Havilland and reporters from the national press. In fact the flight was used as a means of positioning the aircraft to New York so that BOAC could steal a march on its rival by inaugurating simultaneous jet services in both directions across the Atlantic on 4 October 1958. On that date G-APDC commanded by Captain R.E. Millichap, flew London-Gander-New York in 10 hours, 22 minutes, whilst G-APDB under the command of Captain Tom Storey returned from New York in the record time of 6 hours, 11 minutes. The two Comets passed each other in mid-Atlantic and as they neared each other BOAC's Chairman in G-APDC exchanged radio messages with his Managing Director in the other aircraft. The new service was scheduled to operate weekly in each direction but after a few flights had been made it was disrupted by a strike and did not return to a weekly frequency until 13 November. On 13 October the

MTCA published its conditions for permitting Pan-American's Boeing 707s to operate into London Airport. For noise abatement reasons a minimum altitude of 1,000ft had to be attained before flying over built-up areas. At that time this did not pose too much of a problem as the areas under the flight paths for Runways 28R and 28L were not heavily built-up until more than half a mile beyond each runway, and so Pan-American were able to duly introduce 707s onto the London run.

During the winter of 1958/9 fog once again affected many areas of Britain including London. The Central Electricity Generating Board decided to conduct some tests to determine by visual observation whether the efflux gases from its power stations penetrated the fog layer and were dispersed into the upper air. They chartered Dakota G-ALWC from Fairey Surveys for what they christened 'Operation Smoke-Plume'. The Dakota was based at White Waltham airfield in Berkshire, but special advance weather warnings enabled it to be positioned to London Airport on the eve of expected fog conditions. On the afternoon of 3 December 1958 one such warning was received and the aircraft was flown into London Airport. The next morning was one of dense fog and G-ALWC was taxied out to the runway with the aid of the Decca Q-Band ASMI equipment. In visibility officially estimated as well under 300ft the Dakota took off virtually blind and broke into clear sky at 500ft. Photographs were taken of power station chimney gases emerging from the top of the fog layer and the aircraft was then flown back to the airport for a GCA approach. After descending to 200ft without sighting the aircraft's wingtips, let alone the approach lights, the crew diverted to Guernsey, the nearest clear airport. No other aircraft took off or landed at London Airport until late in the evening.

In 1958, the airport complex was considered too large in area to be reached quickly enough from its single fire station. It was thought that two stations would be needed, one on the north side and one in the Central Area. The north side one would be the

Hunting-Clan
Viking
G-AHPJ in the
Central Area.
(Air-Britain)

Iberia
Caravelle
EC-AVZ on
stand in the
Central Area.
(Air-Britain)

Cambrian Airways Dakota G-AGIP on a sparsely populated Central Area apron. (Author)

master station with the Central Area one as its satellite, to reduce demands on space. A satellite fuel station had already been built on the western apex of the Central Area apron, fed from the main fuel farm at Perry Oaks by pipes running beneath the runways and apron. A survey of passengers that year showed that 51 per cent of them used airline coaches to get to the airport, 35 per cent used private cars, 4 per cent came on public buses, and 10 per cent used taxis.

On 20 January 1959, BOAC carried HRH the Duke of Edinburgh out of London in Comet 4 G-APDE on the first stage of his Commonwealth Tour, and on 31 March the airline inaugurated its round-the-world service. Britannia 312 G-AOVT left London to fly to Tokyo and Hong Kong via the Atlantic and Pacific and a day later Comet 4 G-APDH set off for Tokyo via the Eastern Hemisphere route. It arrived on 3 April and commenced its return leg the next day, completing the westbound circuit started by the Britannia. Direct scheduled flights between London and Moscow commenced on 14 May 1959 with BEA Viscounts, and two days later Aeroflot inaugurated TU-104 services. Aerolineas Argentinas replaced the Douglas DC-6s on its Buenos Aires-London route with a twice-weekly Comet 4 operation from 19 May, the first turbo-jet service between South America and the UK. This meant that a regulatory 'jet surcharge' of £4 15s 0d return had to be added to the fare. Prior to this, the piston-engined DC-6s had offered the cheapest tourist-class fare between Buenos Aires and London, at £324 15s 0d return. In June 1959, the UK airline Skyways agreed to lease-purchase four of BOAC's Constellation aircraft, and use them to operate scheduled freight services from London to Hong Kong and Singapore on behalf of BOAC. This contract was to last until 31 March 1962, and the Avro Yorks of Skyways were also often chartered by BOAC and Pan American to ferry replacement engines and spare parts to stranded airliners. In contrast to these ancient types, more new jets continued to be introduced throughout the year. On 27 July, Air France inaugurated Caravelle services into the UK, with F-BHRB opening Nice-London and Paris-London jet services.

Opposite page: A BEA Routemaster bus and baggage trailer outside the Europa Building. (Via David Bowler)

Left: Cunard-Eagle DC-6A G-APSA ready to depart Central Area on a murky day in February 1961. (Steve Bond)

Below: A BEA 'Elizabethan' class Ambassador runs up in the Central Area. In the background are the BEA and BOAC engineering bases. (Air-Britain)

The Canadian company Seaways Hotel Ltd announced plans in 1959 to construct a new £600,000 hotel on a 3.5-acre site on the Bath Road, close to the north side terminal. It was to have 200 rooms, with provision for a further eighty-three to be added, and was to be called the Skyways Hotel. By the beginning of the 1960s, there were in fact two large American-style hotels open on the Bath Road. One was the Ariel Hotel, whose circular shape was said to have been inspired by the Royal Albert Hall. It was sound-proofed and offered courtesy transport to and from the airport terminals. The other, larger, one was the 160-room Skyway Hotel which was opened on 12 January 1960 by the Hon. George A. Drew QC, High Commissioner for Canada. It had a swimming pool and 24-hour restaurant service, and every guest room had a TV and telephone. Within a year a further 100 rooms had been added. One of its first VIP guests was the Italian actress Sophia Loren, who unfortunately had her jewellery stolen from her room while she was eating in the restaurant.

On 7 January 1960, BEA Viscount G-AOHU arrived from Dublin in fog and made a heavy touchdown on runway 28L. Full braking was applied but the nose undercarriage gear failed and the aircraft skidded some 500yds along the runway. A fire broke out in the nose and the aircraft suffered fuselage damage so serious that it had to be written off, but there were no serious injuries among the fifty-four passengers and five crew members. This incident was followed by another mishap on 8 March, when Skyways Hermes G-ALDH landed with six passengers aboard and suffered a collapse of the starboard main undercarriage leg. On 1 April BEA commenced jet operations using Comet 4Bs, the first such service being operated from Tel Aviv to London via Athens and Rome by G-APMB. Other airlines were rapidly switching to jet operations into London, with Pakistan International Airlines introducing a leased Boeing 707 onto their flights from Karachi on 7 March and Air India opening 707 services from Bombay on 19 April, with an extension onwards to New York from 14 May. During April 1960, the Ministry of Aviation approved the plans for a new long-haul terminal in the Central Area and construction commenced. Announcing the go-ahead the Minister of Aviation, Duncan Sandys, said: 'London Airport is Britain's front door. First impressions are important, and the "shantytown" on the north side is to be replaced by an entirely new modern air station.' In May HRH Princess Margaret married Mr Anthony Armstrong-Jones, and on 6 May, five RAF Vulcans set off from London Airport carrying film of the wedding to various commonwealth destinations. More Middle Eastern airlines began to serve London during June. On 15 May the Egyptian airline Misrair commenced a weekly Cairo-Athens-Rome-Geneva-London service with Viscounts. This was upgraded to a five-times-weekly Comet 4C operation from 14 July, and on 20 June Persian Air Services inaugurated the first services from that country to the UK with a twice-weekly Douglas DC-7C schedule.

June 1960 saw the return to service of Runway 28R/10L which had been out of commission since the winter. While it was closed, new lighting was installed and a concrete stub was laid, which would eventually form the basis of a high-speed turn-off. Provision was also made for the eventual installation of red and white visual glide path indicators of the type which had been installed on Runway 28L during the previous summer. The new lighting on 28R/10L included centreline lights and also touchdown zone lighting of the type first used at Gatwick. During the winter of 1960 Runway 28R/10L was scheduled to be taken out of service again during the course of its extension to 11,000ft. While this in progress lighting similar to that on Runway 28L/10R would also be incorporated. In July 1960 the Shell-Mex and BP pipeline supplying fuel to the airport from the depot at Walton-on-Thames was officially opened by Sir Gerard d'Erlanger, Chairman of BOAC. Two 6in pipes ran parallel to each other beneath seventeen roads, two railway lines, the River Thames, and Kempton Park Racecourse before surfacing on the west side of the airport. This was the first such pipeline into any British airport, but delivery of fuel supplies by road tanker still continued as well. In 1959 Shell-Mex and BP had supplied 45 million gallons of fuel to the airport using this method. During the autumn of 1960 sixteen airlines were operating jets into London Airport. These were: Aeroflot (TU-104), Aerolineas Argentinas (Comet 4), Air France (Caravelle), Alitalia (DC-8), BEA (Comet 4B), BOAC (Comet 4 and Boeing 707), East African Airways (Comet 4), Finnair (Caravelle), Olympic Airways (Comet 4B), Pan-American Airways (Boeing 707), QANTAS (Boeing 707), SAS (Caravelle), South African Airways (Boeing 707), Swissair (Caravelle), Trans-Canada Air Lines (DC-8) and Trans World Airlines (Boeing 707).

QANTAS Boeing 707 VH-EBC on the north side, with the terminal buildings and a KLM Viscount in the background. (Air-Britain)

In October 1960, Captain Warren Beall, in command of a Pan-American flight from Frankfurt to London, mistook the gasholder at South Harrow for the similar one at Southall and landed on the 5,400ft runway at RAF Northolt instead of London Airport. The Boeing 707 was brought to a halt with 100yds of runway to spare and the forty-one passengers were transferred to the correct airport by coach. Two hours later Captain Beall ferried the empty aircraft from Northolt to London Airport. He returned to the USA on the same aircraft, but this time as a passenger, and later faced a Pan-American enquiry into the incident. During the month the Ministry of Aviation reduced the number of aircraft permitted on the north side apron from fourteen to eleven because of 'the increased danger of fire from mixture fuels' (the usage of kerosene and JP4 fuels at the same time). Pan-American dismissed this reasoning as 'quite ridiculous'. October 1960 saw some notable lasts at the airport. On 16 October BOAC operated its last scheduled transatlantic service by Comet 4, the routes having been taken over by Boeing 707s, and on the last day of the month BEA operated its last scheduled service by a piston-engined type. On that date, Dakota G-AGZB flew from London Airport to Birmingham under the command of Captain Peter Griffin. The aircraft was sched-uled to operate the return leg as well, but was damaged in the landing at Birmingham and the flight back was cancelled. The occupants of BOAC Boeing 707 G-APFN had a lucky escape on 24 December 1960. The aircraft was making a night approach to Runway 23L under the command of a senior BOAC captain when it touched down almost halfway along the runway. It became clear to the captain that the 707 would not stop in the remaining length of the runway so he attempted to steer it through a right-hand turn onto runway 33L, but the aircraft skidded on the grass and the undercarriage collapsed. There were no injuries amongst the ninety-five passengers and eleven crew members but fuel leakage occurred and the aircraft was substantially damaged. It took five days to move it, during which period the effective length of Runway 05R/23L was reduced to 6,000ft. Runway 28L/10R had already been withdrawn from service while it was being extended and improved and was not due to re-open until March 1961. To add to the problems, the Ministry of Aviation gave notice that Runway 10L/28R, the only serviceable jet runway, would be closed between 7.00a.m. and 8.00a.m. on 29 December for repairs to damage caused by jet efflux lifting tarmac patches.

1961 opened with an announcement in January by Peter Thorneycroft, the Minister of Aviation, that it had been decided to rename London's two major airports 'reflecting the growth of airport traffic at the London airports and their increasing interdepend-ence'. From 1 April 1961 London Airport was to become London (Heathrow) Airport, and Gatwick was to be known as London (Gatwick) Airport. On 21 June 1961 the spectre of a mid-air collision near the airport returned when two London (Heathrow) movements were involved in a near-miss in the London Control Zone about three miles west of Epsom. A United Arab Airlines Comet 4C was inbound from Zurich at

5,000ft and a departing Trans-Canada Air Lines DC-8 was cleared to climb to 4,000ft, but because of a cockpit misunderstanding continued to climb, passing through the Comet's allocated 5,000ft level

A special BOAC Boeing 707 flight on 14 March carried seventy members of the Court of Livery of the Guild of Air Pilots and Air Navigators including their Grand Master HRH the Duke of Edinburgh and escorted by BOAC Chairman Sir Matthew Slattery on a local sortie out of Heathrow, during which the Duke flew the aircraft from the right-hand seat for part of the time. Back on the ground, new parking charges for cars spending more than 48 hours in the Central Area were introduced by the Ministry of Aviation on 20 March 1961. The rates were £1 per day for stays of between two and four days, and £2 per day for stays of over four days, and were to apply until 15 October. It was announced that tenders were shortly to be invited for the construction of a multi-storey car park in the Central Area, but until this was completed passengers who had to leave their cars at the airport for extended periods were advised to apply to the airport management for details of local garages offering parking which included collection from and delivery to the airport. The need for more parking spaces was now apparent, but it had not been foreseen beforehand and as a result valuable parking revenue was being turned away. During March 1961, Runway 10R/28L reopened after its extension to 11,000ft with a 200ft connecting stub on the end to allow further extension.

Beyond the western extremity, work was in progress on culverting the Duke of Northumberland and Longford rivers 300ft to the west, to reduce the hazards to any aircraft over-running the extended runway. In the course of repair work during the winter some 1,700 concrete pit covers, each several inches thick, had been replaced by special ones bound with iron. It had been found that during the first full year of big jet operations very severe runway wear had occurred and the pit covers were cracking under the repeated landing impacts. In June 1961, the Ministry of Aviation announced that a new arrangement permitting fully equipped multi-engined private and execu-tive aircraft flown by instrument-rated pilots to land at London Heathrow was to come into effect forthwith for a trial period of three months. Blackout periods would apply during peak hours, these totalling 4 hours daily for domestic flights and 6 hours daily for international flights. A blackout period would also apply during public holidays and for one week before and after. It was made clear that the new arrangements did not mean that the airport was available for recreational or pleasure flying. Light aircraft flying into the airport were required to use the special call-sign prefix 'Cigar'. The first aircraft to take advantage of the ruling was a single-engined Mooney 21 demonstration aircraft on delivery to R.K. Dundas Ltd. This was flown non-stop across the Atlantic from Boston by the highly experienced ferry pilot Walter Moody and arrived at Heathrow on 1 July 1961. During 1961, BEA's Chairman, Lord Douglas of Kirtleside, said that the airline was willing to contribute up to £1 million towards the cost of a monorail link with the centre of London. BEA preferred the monorail option over improved road links because the volume of road traffic had a tendency to quickly catch up with any additional road capacity, and the airline considered that road traffic may in the future be a limiting factor in city centre to city centre timings as the introduction of automatic landing permitted higher flight frequencies.

On 13 November 1961, the first half of the new long-haul terminal building in the Central Area came into partial operation when passengers on a BOAC Comet flight were the first to use it, the new building being initially reserved for BOAC and the other airlines it handled at the airport. As a temporary measure arriving passengers were routed through part of the short-haul terminal, and rival airlines would have to continue to use the north side facilities until the whole complex was completed. The new building was situated on the south-west side of the Central Area, but some distance outside of the diamond-shaped area originally envisaged. In its finished form it was to consist of a rectangular passenger building measuring 430ft by 280ft and connected by a covered footbridge to two office blocks, each 410ft by 55ft, which housed airline offices and other facilities. Work was already in hand on the flanking southern block, and was scheduled to start shortly on the northern one. The height of the terminal complex

BOAC VC-10 G-ARVB on lease to Nigeria Airways at the Oceanic Building, with an Iraqui Airways Trident in the background. (Maurice Marsh)

was restricted to two storeys to avoid obstruction of the view of the apron from the new control tower. In February 1962 seven Ministry of Aviation apron staff received new BEA cap badges marking the first stage of BEA's eventual takeover of apron services in the Central Area. During the financial year 1961/2 the airport made a profit of £750,000, a major improvement on the previous year's £80,000 loss. On 28 March 1962, the north side passenger terminal was closed to scheduled airline traffic and the remaining airlines transferred their operations to the new long-haul terminal in the Central Area. However, the Royal Suite remained on the north side, and as well as VIP flights the north side apron was still used for cargo operations and for aircraft parking until the late 1960s.

During May 1962 test pilot 'Dizzy' Addicott carried out wet runway braking trials at the airport using Supermarine Swift F.7 XF114. He used No.1 runway for the trials, typically touching down at 180mph just before a 300ft stretch of runway which had been specially flooded with 600 gallons of water. He reported experiencing 'little or no apparent loss of speed' until reaching the dry area of the runway. In 1962 Heathrow was the leading airport in Europe, handling 6.95 million passengers on 156,085 flights, but by March of that year it was struggling to cope with the volume of cars. The car parking situation had become desperate, with the existing capacity of 2,500 cars proving to be totally insufficient, and so work started that summer on a new multi-storey car park on the south-west side of the Central Area. The work was scheduled for completion in the spring of 1963 and would require the temporary closure of the existing Central Area car park. Alterations were also planned to relieve the passenger congestion in No.1 and No.2 Terminals. Two fingers, each 600-700ft long, were to be added to No.1 Terminal at a cost of between £150,000 and £175,000 each, with completion of the first being scheduled for September 1963. At that time interest in a rail link into central London was waning as by the end of 1964 the new Chiswick-Langley motorway would be in operation and would have a spur cutting southwards under the Bath Road and virtually into the Central Area. During the period 3-6 December 1962 Heathrow was closed due to thick 'smog' (fog mixed with industrial air pollution). Luton Airport remained fully operational however, and so KLM operated its Amsterdam-London Lockheed Electra services through Luton, as did Aer Lingus with its Viscount and Dakota services from Dublin. To process these diversions HM Customs officers and immigration officials were sent over to Luton from Heathrow.

On 3 February 1963 BEA's new three-storey catering building , capable of producing 8,000 meals per day, was opened on the north side of the airport. Another occupant of the north side area was the British independent airline BKS Air Transport. They transferred their operations department from Southend to Building 224 on the north side apron on 15 February 1963. In the summer their London reservations department also moved across. At that time BKS were selling over 2,300 seats per week, using 'sell and record' charts in those pre-computer days. Their office was equipped with the new 'key and lamp' telephone system. On 8 February 1963, the airport had a visit from what was then the largest airliner in the world, Tupolev Tu-114 CCCP-76481. The giant turbo-prop aircraft had been chartered by from Aeroflot tycoon Roy Thomson to take 170 British businessmen on a trade mission to Moscow, bringing them back three days later. BEA handled the flights and had to rig two sets of aircraft steps together to reach the doors of the Tupolev. On 1 April 1963, the first Rail-Air link to the airport was inaugurated. Passengers from the Midlands and the north-west of England travelled by rail to Watford Junction station, where a connecting coach took them onwards to Heathrow. In 1965 the scheme would be extended to meet the needs of passengers from the south-west of England with a coach link from Reading station. On 20 August 1963, travellers by car had their load lightened somewhat by the opening of the first multi-storey car park in the Central Area, offering 1,063 spaces.

On 6 November 1963, Trans-Canada Air Lines Douglas DC-8 CF-TJM, operating flight AC861 to Montreal, aborted its take-off from runway 28R in thick fog because of a suspected elevator control problem. The aircraft overran the runway and came to rest in a cabbage patch about 800yds further on. There were only minor injuries among the ninety passengers and seven crew members, but because of the fog it took the fire and rescue services some time to locate the aircraft, which was eventually repaired and returned to service. From early May in 1964 parallel landing and take-off procedures were trialled at Heathrow. Initially, these procedures were only applied when the cloudbase was at 350ft or more and the visibility was in excess of five miles. In June of that year construction group Taylor Woodrow announced its decision to enter into the development of suspended passenger vehicles, and took out a UK licence for the SAFEGE 'Metro Suspendu' system. One application considered for the vehicles was a link between Heathrow and Victoria Station in London. This would cost three to six times less than an underground rail link and could carry up to 40,000 passengers each way every hour. The developed SAFEGE carriages would make the eighteen-mile journey in just over 10 minutes, at 100mph.

In February 1964 almost 4,000 screaming female fans thronged the roof terraces of the Queen's Building to welcome home the Beatles pop group from their tour of the USA and to see them disembark from their Pan-American Boeing 707. BEA's new Trident jet was officially christened by Lady Douglas pouring a bottle of champagne over the nose of G-ARPG in a ceremony at the airport on 28 February. This example also went on to operate BEA's first Trident revenue service when it was substituted for a Comet 4B on a morning London-Copenhagen flight on 11 March. The Fairey Company's long-running compensation battle was finally settled on 13 May 1964 when it was awarded £527,781 of its original £1.8 million claim against the Ministry of Aviation for the loss of its Great West Aerodrome. The Ministry had proposed a £235,227 settlement. The

Lands Tribunal awarded Fairey £320,570 in respect of freehold lands and buildings requisitioned during the Second World War when the original plans for London Airport were drawn up. A further £157,211 was awarded in respect of the rental of lands and buildings from November 1943, when the 240-acre aerodrome was requisitioned, until June 1960 when agreement was finally reached on the compulsory purchase of the property. Following the settlement the former Fairey hangar in the Central Area, the last survivor of the airport's original buildings, was demolished in 1964. By the mid-1960s the short-haul terminal was divided into No.1 Building 'Europa', used for services to continental Europe, and the smaller No.2 Building 'Britannic', used for domestic movements. The 'Europa' building was itself subdivided into areas for inbound and outbound traffic. The more distant stands still had to be accessed by buses, although piers were being built to increase the number of stands with direct access from the terminal. The first such airbridges were introduced by BEA on services to Paris on 16 November 1965. On the same date, BEA's new Motor Transport Base on the north side of the airport came into operation. This incorporated a fully equipped servicing depot for ground equipment and a control centre to co-ordinate vehicle movements and requirements. On 1 August BEA had introduced its Executive Express coach service. For a fare of 10s one-way (twice the price of the normal airport coach) passengers with hand baggage only on peak-hour services from Aberdeen, Edinburgh, Glasgow and Belfast were met by the coach at the foot of the aircraft steps and transferred directly from the tarmac to the airline's West London Air Terminal.

The first Royal flight in a Vickers VC-10 took place in February 1965 when BOAC example G-ARVL carried HM the Queen and the Duke of Edinburgh on a tour of Ethiopia and the Sudan. Services by the larger Super VC-10 were inaugurated by BOAC-Cunard on 1 April 1965 when G-ASGD operated a service to New York. BEA Trident 1 G-ARPR made history on 10 June 1965 when it made the world's first Autoflare automatic touchdown at the conclusion of flight BE343 from Paris (Le Bourget) to Heathrow. Although the landing was carried out in good visibility as a precaution, it was still an important step along the road to fully automatic landings. Had such a landing aid been fully operational on 27 October 1965 it might have prevented the tragic loss of BEA Vanguard G-APEE. This aircraft was inbound to Heathrow on a late night service from Edinburgh with thirty passengers and six crew members. Visibility at Heathrow was poor and the crew made two abortive attempts to land on Runway 28R before joining the stack of aircraft holding at the Garston holding point. After 30 minutes or so, during which another Vanguard had landed successfully and another had to overshoot, the crew commenced another monitored approach to Runway 28R. Three quarters of a mile from the runway threshold they attempted a go-around but the Vanguard entered a steep dive and struck the runway about 2,600ft in from the threshold at 1.23a.m. All on board perished.

Lufthansa Viscount D-ANOL in the Central Area in the early 1960s. In the background are BEA Viscounts and Dakotas and a Comet 4B. (Via Author)

By 1965 the long-haul terminal building was officially known as No.3 Building 'Oceanic'. For the benefit of those seeing off passengers, a 'waving base' ran the full length of the face overlooking the apron, and a viewing area on the roof afforded a clear view through glass into the final departure lounge. It was proposed that a small admission charge to this area be introduced, partly to provide a source of revenue for the airport and partly to control the numbers using the area at any one time. Inside the terminal a nursery with playroom, cots and baby feeding cubicles was provided, with qualified nurses on duty from 8.00a.m. to 10.00p.m.. On the first floor was a quick-service restaurant and cocktail bar, with the main restaurant and another cocktail bar in the southern annexe block for the time being. Escalators were not provided in the terminal, as the rise between the two floors was only 13ft, and a surprisingly high number of complaints had been received about those in the short-haul terminal. The VIP suite was to be located under the finger leading to the north office block and on special occasions such as a visit by a head of state spectators were to be allowed access to the roof area to view the proceedings through glass. The long-haul terminal was to be renamed Terminal 3 in 1968.

On 1 April 1966 control of the airport passed to the state-owned British Airports Authority under the chairmanship of Peter Masefield. The name of the airport was changed again, to Heathrow Airport (London) and as part of the ceremony some thirty-year-old trees were planted in the Central Area, hopefully to provide instant blossom.

Two BOAC–Cunard Boeing 707s on the apron at the Oceanic Building. (Maurice Marsh)

Above: A tarmac scene outside the Oceanic Building, featuring Boeing 707s of Pan American, TWA, QANTAS and Air India. (Via Author)

A BOAC-Cunard Boeing 707 and Middle East Airlines Comet 4C OD-ADT at the Oceanic Building. (Maurice Marsh)

A view of the Central Area complex including the uncompleted Queen's Building, taken from the top of the tunnel entrance. (John Carter)

A view looking north from the top of the Queen's Building in 1959, showing the tunnel entrance, the ground-level car parks and the future site of Terminal One. (Clive Dyball)

The north side apron was still being used on special occasions, and on 18 May 1966, after lengthy delays, aviatrix Miss Sheila Scott finally set off from there in her single-engined Piper Commanche 260 G-ATOY at 4.55p.m. for Rome, on the first leg of her 30,000-mile solo round-the-world flight. She arrived back at Heathrow on 20 June 1966 after a successful circumnavigation of the globe during which she set many point to point records en route. At this time urgent talks were ongoing with British Rail over the long-proposed spur line extension from Feltham into the airport to enable non-stop services from Victoria station to be operated. Such measures were needed to cope with the relentless expansion in services from Heathrow. In 1966 it was the world's seventh-busiest airport in terms of total aircraft movements, which totalled 224,086, carrying around 11.9 million passengers.

Early in 1967, BOAC drew up its own plans for the proposed development of its own premises at Heathrow. These included the construction of its own passenger terminal, near to its engineering base and to the north and east of the Eagle Airways hangars. To serve this terminal a new road from Hatton Cross into the Central Area would need to be constructed. The Underground rail line would need to be extended from Hounslow West to enter the airport at Hatton Cross, make a stop at the proposed BOAC terminal and then continue onwards to the Central Area and Perry Oaks, where the BAA had plans for its own new passenger terminal. The proposed British Rail spur line from Feltham was also intended to enter the airport near Hatton Cross and follow the Underground route into the Central Area, swinging south after Perry Oaks to serve a proposed new cargo terminal. In the end the BAA rejected BOAC's proposal because it would have meant the closure of No.2 runway and the construction of a replacement runway to the west of the airport. The BAA also had plans for a small terminal, similar to the one at Gatwick, to handle the increasing number of executive aircraft movements at Heathrow. Two sites were considered, one on the north side and the other on the south side where the Field's hangar was situated and where the aircraft of Shell and Granada TV already operated from. In March 1967, BEA Helicopters was planning to re-open helicopter services between Heathrow and central London, this time using twenty-six-seater Sikorsky S-61s. The

Air Transport Licensing Board had already granted a ten-year licence to take effect on 1 January 1968 and the Port of London Authority had given verbal approval for a 58,000 sq.ft. floating helipad on the Thames, close to the east side of Waterloo Bridge. The plans still needed approval from Lambeth Borough Council, but BEA was considering a frequency of around twenty-two flights each day, to be adjusted to match the frequency of its fixed-wing services through Heathrow. The fare was to be in the region of £3 each way. The 16 May 1967 saw BEA Trident G-ARPP make the world's first fully automated landing by an aircraft operating a scheduled passenger service. On arrival at Heathrow from Nice, each of the passengers was presented with a commemorative tie or neckscarf.

At midnight on 8 December 1967, a 48-hour total work stoppage by BOAC pilots came into effect, causing the cancellation of thirty-two flights out of Heathrow and the transfer of around 900 passengers to rival airlines. The strike was the first ever official strike action to be called by BALPA, the pilots' trade union, and cost BOAC nearly £500,000 in lost revenue. More disruption occurred during the night of 8-9 January 1968 when the south of England suffered moderate to severe snowfalls with local drifting. Heathrow was closed from 3.10a.m. until 11.01a.m. on 9 January, and on 10 January operations were considerably restricted because snow, slush and surface water on the runways, taxiways and aprons froze solid. This prevented aircraft from taxying and hampered the safe movement of tractors, airport buses and pedestrians on the apron. Because the freezing conditions persisted for several days the ice hazard was responsible for more delays than the original snowfall. The airlines had trouble keeping their aircraft free of ice and one airline ran out of de-icing fluid. On the evening of 8 January sleet and slush had been forecast and the decision had been taken to keep the 9,311ft Runway 28R/10L clear rather than the 12,000ft Runway 28L/10R. In the event, it was thickly falling snow that arrived instead. Clearance work on the shorter runway had begun when the snow started, and when it was realised that it was going to be of significant proportions the decision was taken to keep on clearing 28R/10L rather than start from scratch on the other runway. This meant that on the following day only the shorter runway was operational restricting the take-off weights of some flights. Several airlines complained about this and also about the fact that the taxiways and aprons were not cleared quickly enough in their opinion. The equipment available at that time included five blower/sweepers, four rotary snowploughs and twelve conventional ones, six brushers and five gritters, although the last mentioned had to be used with caution because of the danger of grit ingestion into the turbines of aircraft engines.

In February 1968 the BAA announced its plans for coping with the wide-bodied Boeing 747 when it began using Heathrow in 1969 (in fact the first arrival was not to be until 21 January 1970). It was proposed to close Runway 33L/15R and build a new pier system starting at the Oceanic Building and ending in a series of forward lounges on the site of that runway. A new long-haul arrivals building was to be built adjacent to the Oceanic Building, which would then be used solely for departures. The whole long-haul terminal complex was to be renamed Terminal 3, and the estimated cost of the redevelopment was to be in excess of £10 million, which included an order for twenty-one telescopic jetties from Babcock Moxey of London worth in excess of £900,000. In order to maintain its levels of foreign currency earnings after a devaluation of the pound sterling the BAA also announced an increase in landing fees for international flights to take effect from 1 April 1968. Long-haul charges would increase by 16.66 per cent and medium-haul charges by 12.5 per cent. The British airlines promptly protested that they would end up paying more than their foreign rivals, because the increases for overseas airlines would be offset by the effects of the devaluation. A US-operated Boeing 707 flight would still end up paying the same US$581 after devaluation had been taken into account, whereas the fee for a BOAC VC-10 flight would increase from £221 to £258. However, it was not just the UK airlines that were disgruntled. At a meeting of the Heathrow Airport Airline Operators Committee in April 1968, forty of the forty-three airlines present voted to reject the increases and to withhold the amount of the increases when making their payments to the BAA.

During 1968 two major accidents occurred in full view of passengers and spectators at the airport. On 8 April BOAC Boeing 707 G-ARWE departed for Zurich at 3.27p.m. on the first leg of flight BA712 to Sydney. Twenty seconds after take-off the crew felt and heard a combined shock and bang and a serious fire developed in the No.2 engine. They turned back for Heathrow and an intended emergency landing on runway 05R. About 1.5 minutes after the fire broke out, the No.2 engine and part of its pylon separated from the wing and fell into a water-filled gravel pit. A landing was made on Runway 05R and the passengers were evacuated as the aircraft burnt out. Four passengers did not escape the flames and perished. Twenty-two-year-old air hostess Barbara Jane Harrison died whilst trying to help a disabled passenger out of the aircraft and was posthumously awarded the George Cross, becoming its youngest recipient. Also decorated was Chief Steward Neville Davis-Gordon, who received the BEM for Gallantry (Civil Division) for his efforts. Another aircraft was lost on 3 July 1968. Airspeed Ambassador G-AMED of BKS Air Transport had been specially converted for the carriage of livestock and was bringing a consignment of horses into Heathrow on a charter flight from Deauville. As it was approaching the threshold of Runway 28R it suffered a fatigue failure of the port flap actuating rod, causing the port flap to retract. The port wing dropped suddenly and an uncontrollable rolling movement to port developed. The wingtip and the port main landing gear made contact with the grass to the left of the runway and the aircraft slewed across the grass, striking two parked BEA Tridents before bursting into flames, rolling onto its back and coming to rest against the ground floor of the partially constructed new Terminal One. All eight occupants of the Ambassador and its cargo of horses were killed. The tail was sliced off BEA Trident

G-ARPT which had to be written off, Trident G-ARPI was severely damaged but eventually repaired, and damage was also sustained by BEA Viscount G-APJU, which was loaded with passengers and about to depart for the Channel Islands.

In April 1968 St George's Chapel in the middle of the Central Area was approaching completion but still needed funds to enable it to be finished. A donation of 500 guineas was received from the BAA, but that still left a shortfall of some £20,000 to be made up. However, this was found, and the chapel was completed in October 1968. Work had begun in 1967 on a plot of land to one side of the control tower. The chapel was located completely underground, with just its tall cross visible at ground level. It was intended for the use of all passengers and airport workers of all faiths, having three altars and services conducted by clergy of differing faiths at different times of day. In September 1968, the BAA had capital works in hand at all its airports at a total cost of nearly £37 million. Nearly all of this was at Heathrow, which had by then become the busiest international airport in the world in terms of passengers handled, being 45 per cent up on its nearest rival, New York's J. F. Kennedy Airport. On 11 December 1968, the inward (eastern) bore of the tunnel into the Central Area had to be temporarily closed to traffic. Tests carried out by the BAA in conjunction with the Road Research Laboratory had shown that part of the roof lining was not adhering to the tunnel shell. Although there was no danger of the actual tunnel structure collapsing, there was a threat of debris from the roof lining falling onto tunnel users. The initial traffic chaos was alleviated by using the cargo tunnel for airline vehicles and passengers' cars and by allowing light vehicles to use the cycle tracks in the main tunnel.

Despite its massive expansion in services Heathrow still occasionally made room for light aircraft movements, none lighter than the home-built Jodel D.9 G-AVPD. This had been constructed by BEA employee Stuart McKay and was housed in a corner of the BEA engineering base prior to its first flight. Because the Jodel had no wheel brakes, a special grass strip, named for the occasion runway 28L Special, was mown on Block 14 just to the right of runway 28L and delineated with rubber markers. On 14 June 1969, G-AVPD was granted a special Visual Flight Rules clearance and was taken into the air for the first time by Captain John Ellis for the 22-minute ferry flight to nearby Booker Aerodrome.

7

TERMINAL ONE

In May 1966 the civil engineering group Tersons was announced as the main contractor for the new passenger terminal to be built on the northeast side of the Central Area. The new building was to have two piers with twenty-one forward waiting-rooms along their length. Telescopic bridges were to provide direct access from the piers to the doors of waiting aircraft. It was to have its own multi-storey car park and two coach stations, and the total cost of the project was estimated at £6.9 million. Planning had actually commenced in 1964 to the design of Frederick Gibberd and Partners, their third terminal building project at Heathrow. The terminal was designed to be brought into operation in two stages. The first stage was scheduled for completion in late 1968 and was to cater for passengers on domestic flights and services to Ireland and the Channel Islands. The second stage was intended for completion in the spring of 1969, when the international services of BEA and the airlines it handled would be transferred from the Europa Building, although BEA would still retain a handling unit there to handle airlines such as Swissair, Aeroflot, and Icelandair.

Terminal One, as the new short-haul terminal was named, opened to the public on 6 November 1968. At the time it was the largest airline terminal in Europe in terms of space, passenger capacity and number of boarding gates. With its opening the Europa Building was renamed Terminal Two, and absorbed the facilities of the Britannic Building. The temporary arrivals building under No.2 car park was discontinued, and Terminal Two was remodelled to suit the requirements of the non-UK short-haul airlines. Terminal One was constructed on two levels, with all arriving passengers entering the building on the ground floor and all departing passengers going directly to the first floor. The terminal was designed on a 'long and narrow' principle, with an extensive frontage for vehicle

Terminal One – standing for Number One service

The brand new Terminal 1 at London Airport is the centre of BEA's Inter-Britain network and from early summer it will also be used for our International flights. Here you can change planes for destinations all over the country, quickly and conveniently in complete comfort. With everything necessary for a smooth transit laid on under one roof. Terminal One is the most modern, most advanced passenger terminal in Europe. It's symbolic of the Number One service that's standard with BEA, Europe's Number One airline.

BEA

No.1 in Europe

1969 BEA timetable advertisement for the new Terminal 1. (Via Author)

setting down or picking up passengers and with a narrow depth to reduce the walking distance from the front entrance to the parked aircraft. These were accessed via two piers, No.4 with eight stands for domestic services, and No.3 which would eventually handle international flights using twelve stands. The stands could be used for nose-in loading by most types of aircraft, one notable exception being the Viscount. Terminal One was designed to cope with 900 domestic passengers and 1,450 international passengers in each direction every hour, thus increasing the total capacity of the airport by about two-thirds. It incorporated 120 closed-circuit television screens linked to the BEACON computer at the West London Air Terminal, and displaying up-to-the-minute flight information. One airline which did not survive to use the new terminal was British Eagle International Airlines, which ceased operations on the very day that the new building came into service. The redundant British Eagle fleet remained parked up at their Heathrow engineering base for several months before disposal, and Blocks 41 and 44 continued to be referred to as the 'Eagle taxiway' for several years afterwards.

Terminal One was officially opened by HM the Queen on 17 April 1969 when she unveiled a commemorative plaque. At that time it was still only handling domestic services, with about 7,000 passengers passing through each day, but from 7 May 1969 it began to accept international flights, beginning with the arrival of a flight from Palma at 6.35a.m. On that date BKS Air Transport, Cambrian Airways, Autair, Aer Lingus and Cyprus Airways transferred their operations across. Twenty gates were now served by piers, with buses being used to transfer passengers to other, remote stands. One of the outstanding interior features of the terminal was a 28ft by 5ft mural painted by William Dempster and depicting pioneer British airlines and some of the people who kept them operating. On 25 June 1969 Westward Airways inaugurated a shuttle service between Heathrow and Gatwick using Britten-Norman Islander aircraft. Up to six flights a day in each direction were operated, linking the two airports in around 15 minutes' flying time, compared to an average journey time of 1.5 hours by road. By August of that year Terminal One was handling around 25,000 passengers each day, out of the total airport figure of around 59,000.

8

THE ENGINEERING BASES

Between 1947 and 1950 eight temporary steel hangars, each of about 100ft span, were erected for BOAC and used for a large part of its maintenance programme. Hangars 2, 3 and 4 faced Runway 23, while hangar 1, just to the north of them, had its doors facing on a more southerly aspect. By 1949 there was insufficient space at Northolt for BEA's needs and the decision was taken to transfer operations to Heathrow at the earliest opportunity. In May BEA announced that its forthcoming fleet of 'Elizabethan' class Airspeed Ambassadors would be based at Heathrow, where a new maintenance base for them and other future types would be constructed. In August 1951, the airline announced that pending completion of the first bays of its new engineering base it would probably move into part of the large aluminium alloy hangar which had recently been completed in No.2 maintenance area. The plan for the Central Area complex specified three areas to be used as maintenance areas. The first, No.1 maintenance area, covered over 240 acres adjacent to the Great South West Road. It contained several temporary steel hangars and was earmarked for the future BEA engineering base and the BOAC maintenance area which would also incorporate the airline's new headquarters building. No.2 maintenance area occupied over 70 acres and was intended for the use of foreign operators and the British independent airlines. The first building to be erected there (after shipment in parts from the USA) was a large permanent steel hangar for Pan-American Airways. This was 160ft wide and 122ft deep, with a 'tail-gate' 20ft wide by 12ft high at the front to enable Stratocruisers to be accommodated. Also in this area was a three-bay hangar built mainly of aluminium alloy, the first hangar of such construction in the world and the first permanent hangar to be built from scratch at the airport. The first bay of the still incomplete hangar was opened by BOAC Chairman Sir Miles Thomas in May 1951 and it was complete by August of that year. It was used by the BOAC Comet 1 fleet, but by 1954 it had been taken over by Hunting-Clan Air Transport. After that airline was merged with Airwork to form British United Airways it was used by Seaboard and Western as a freight transit shed. A further 90-acre site, earmarked as No.3 maintenance area, was held in reserve to meet future engineering needs.

During 1950 and 1951, BOAC maintained all its aircraft types at London Airport with the exception of its new Stratocruiser and Constellation fleets. These were still looked after at Filton near Bristol whilst work was in progress on BOAC's new engineering base and headquarters building, but as the construction progressed Constellation maintenance was transferred across to hangars 2, 3 and 4 in 1953, and in October 1954 the Stratocruisers moved into the south-east hangars. During 1952 BOAC's Hermes aircraft were retired and replaced by Canadair Argonauts. The Hermes fleet was cocooned at the London Airport base pending sale. Four examples were sold to the Britavia group but the BOAC engineers refused to work on re-commissioning them 'until satisfactory assurances have been obtained that they will not be engaged on work which could be undertaken by BOAC'. The first stage of the new BOAC complex was opened in 1955, the BOAC headquarters officially transferring across from Airways House in Brentford on 11 July. Four storeys of offices housed most of BOAC's training, operations, supplies and administrative staff, who nicknamed it the 'Kremlin'. The second floor was reserved for the directors, and was the only floor to be carpeted. On the third floor room B314 was converted into a writing room for the use of captains passing through the airport. Another new storey was erected nearby to house the accounts, catering, catering and provisioning, and cabin crew training departments. The headquarters building incorporated four large hangars and a complete engine workshop. These were constructed of reinforced concrete and featured two very long cantilevers, each supported on two concrete pylons giving uninterrupted door openings of 300ft. The engineering workshop was 800ft long and 90ft deep. Work commenced immediately on the second stage of the engineering base, which became known as the 'Britannia hangar' and housed the simulator for that type. The second stage came into operation in 1957. At the beginning of 1958, eight BOAC Constellations could be seen at the base, cocooned and awaiting sale. By 1959 the BOAC Movement Control Room was also housed at the airport. Large boards on the walls displayed details of all aircraft in service on the route network. Beside the chalked-up details of each flight was a white light which was illuminated all the time that flight was airborne. In the centre of the circular room was a large horizontal map of the world on which small model aircraft showed the location of all BOAC flights at that moment in time. A small number of adult visitors (usually limited to thirty) were allowed to visit the premises and were shown around on every day except Sundays. By the mid-1960s around 5,000 people were employed in the new headquarters building, about a quarter of BOAC's total staff worldwide.

The newly built BOAC administration block in the mid-1950s. (Via Author)

BOAC Britannia 102 G-ANBB outside their engineering base. (Air-Britain)

British Eagle
Britannia 312
G-AOVK outside
their engineering
base. (Air-Britain)

British Eagle
Britannia 312
G-AOVE minus
titles outside the
BOAC engineering
base. (Air-Britain)

Retired BOAC
Argonaut G-ALHJ
I outside their
engineering base
while being used for
apprentice training.
(Author)

Hunting-Clan Avro York G-AMUU outside the Pan American hangar on the south side. (Air-Britain)

Two BOAC Comet 4s and a Stratocruiser at the BOAC engineering base in May 1960. (Clive Dyball)

Above: BOAC Britannia 102 G-ANBH at the airline's engineering base in November 1959. (Clive Dyball)

Left: Comet 4 G-APDN at the BOAC engineering base in May 1960. (Clive Dyball)

In 1952, BEA had just one small hangar on the south side of the airport. To get to this from the north side terminal complex aircraft had to taxi through the massive Central Area construction site, a convoluted journey of several miles. Work on a new engineering base at the airport had begun in July 1950 and on 17 March 1952 BEA commenced the transfer of its facilities and equipment from Northolt. The move was officially completed on 17 April, although some electrical and instrument workshops remained at Northolt for some time afterwards, and there were some initial problems arising from poor public transport access and lack of canteen facilities to be overcome at the new location. The new engineering base comprised two long hangars arranged back to back, and behind this were located workshops and stores. Each hangar was equipped with an overhead crane and contained a unique system of permanent maintenance bays, each one self-contained and consisting of a series of platforms and decks providing easy access to all parts of an aircraft. The base cost £2 million and was used initially by Elizabethan and Viscount aircraft only, with Viking and Pionair maintenance being carried out at Renfrew Airport, Glasgow. The first five bays came into service in 1952, followed by a further five the following year. In October 1956, work commenced on a new extension that would double the floor area to 958,000 square feet. Completion was scheduled for 1960, in time to handle the new fleet of Vickers Vanguards. During the late 1950s the BEA engineering base was also a popular venue for guided visits by school parties and aviation enthusiasts groups. During the financial year 1958-9, 5,250 people were shown around. By the mid-1960s the base consisted of two large buildings containing twenty maintenance bays. There were also two engine testbeds, and the staff numbered over 4,000. On 19 May 1960 the hangar block extension was handed over by Lord Ashcombe, Chairman of Holland and Hannen and Cubitts, to BEA's chairman, Lord Douglas. Once the office blocks were completed later that year the engineering base would cover 65 acres, with a floor area of 23,000 sq. ft. In October 1961 BEA engineers carried out their last overhaul of a BEA Dakota. To mark the occasion an affectionate 'memorial tribute' ceremony was held at the Heathrow engineering base.

BOAC Comet 4s inside Technical Block B at the BOAC engineering base. (Eric Loseby)

BOAC Constellation G-AHEK undergoes an engine change by the night shift in No.3 Hangar at the BOAC engineering base. (Eric Loseby)

Above left: An aerial view of the BOAC engineering base and partly constructed admin building in June 1962. (Clive Dyball)

Above right: A World Wide Aviation DC-4 at the Eagle Airways hangars. (Frank Hudson)

QANTAS Constellation VH-EAN at Hangar No.3 at the BOAC engineering base. (Eric Loseby)

A Skyways Constellation outside the BOAC hangars in the 1950s. (Eric Loseby)

Stratocruiser G-ANUB at the BOAC engineering base in November 1959. (Eric Loseby)

Meanwhile, back in 1952, Smiths Aircraft Instruments held a party in Hut 204D in the No.1 maintenance area on 14 October to launch their new 'over the counter' component service at the airport. For the past two years Smiths had been using the hut for the overhaul of the autopilots installed in BOAC Comet and Hermes aircraft, and they hoped to eventually offer a similar service to the many overseas airlines using London Airport. Another new service facility opened for business in February 1957 when the Minister of Transport and Civil Aviation, Harold Watkinson, officially opened the new Rolls-Royce aero service building situated to the south-east of the BEA engineering base. This centre went on to provide spares support for the Rolls-Royce engines used by all the airlines at the airport. Cunard-Eagle Airways took delivery of their first Boeing 707 at their engineering base at the airport on 30 April 1962 and held a press reception to mark the event in a marquee pitched nearby. At this reception the airline's Chairman Harold Bamberg announced that 34 acres of land close to the airline's base had been earmarked for expansion, and if Ministry approval was forthcoming it was hoped to develop the site with new terminals for both passengers and cargo. Early in 1967 BOAC submitted plans for the development of its Heathrow base. These included three new hangars to be sited in a line westwards from near the western corner of the most northerly of the existing two BOAC technical blocks, to handle the new wide-bodied Boeing 747 fleet. Approval was received for these buildings and also for a new road to run from Hatton Cross through the BOAC engineering base and into the Central Area.

9

THE CARGO AREAS

In September 1946, BSAA was handling its cargo in one half of a large green corrugated hut near the control tower, the other half of which later became the Green Dragon canteen. The floor was marked out into squares, into which was placed the cargo for a particular flight, sometimes as many as six packages, and a marker board bearing the flight number. There was no heating, and former employee Keith Hayward recalled trying to reconcile freight labels with cargo manifests during the winter and having to brush snow off the labels in order to read them. During 1946, 2,386 tons of cargo passed through the airport. In December 1949, planning had begun for a separate freight area to the north of the western end of No. 1 runway, but for many years to come freight flights were to share the north side apron with passenger services. By 1953 the cargo total for the year had risen to 17,140 tons, which was 60 per cent of the air freight handled by all the London area airports. In August 1957 the Millbourn Report on London Airport included a recommendation that a new freight building be constructed in the Central Area to the left of the tunnel entrance. Before this could come about, in June 1961 Seaboard and Western Airlines transferred all its cargo activities to a new site on the south side of the airport. This facility had a floor area of 18,000 sq. ft and was opened in preparation for the airline's introduction of Canadair CL-44 turboprop 'swing-tail' freighters the following month. By December 1961 the lifting of import restrictions resulted in large numbers of American-built light aircraft being airfreighted into the UK, usually aboard London-bound DC-7F freighters of BOAC and Pan-American and the CL-44s of Seaboard and Western. One of the major customers was Vigors Aviation, the UK agent for Piper aircraft types. All of their stock of Piper Colt trainers had been airfreighted in, and they were shortly to start receiving examples of the new Piper Cherokee by the same method. From 29 October 1962 all of BOAC's export cargo passed through a new 60,000 sq. ft warehouse which had been erected by the Ministry of Aviation on a site near the No.3 passenger terminal in the Central Area. Prior to its opening, BOAC cargo had to be transported to the Central Area by road from a warehouse on the north side apron. In March 1963, Trans-Canada Air Lines inaugurated all-cargo jet services to London with Douglas DC-8Fs, and on 17 June Pan-American replaced its DC-7F freighters with thirteen-pallet Boeing 707-321Cs on the New York-London route. The services operated on every day except Mondays, and each 707 had a freight capacity of 42 tons.

Left: Two Bell 47 helicopters (minus their tail booms) shortly after being air-freighted into the north side apron in July 1961. (Frank Hudson via airliners.net)

Below: Piper Colt G-ARNC has just been air-freighted in and waits to be roaded onwards from the north side apron in June 1961. (Frank Hudson via airliners.net)

One of the RSPA transit hostel's many visitors is visited by a BUA hostess. (Vic Attwood)

By 1964 the BEA Air Cargo Unit at Heathrow was the largest of its kind in the world and the only one offering a complete air cargo service 24 hours a day, 365 days a year. The Ministry had plans for a new permanent cargo centre on the south-west side of the airport in the No. 3 maintenance area, but this was not going to be ready until 1967-8, so in the meantime BOAC and BEA agreed to collaborate on the development of an interim cargo base within BOAC's No. 1 maintenance area, to be operational by the end of the year.

In June 1966, Taylor Woodrow Construction was appointed main contractor for the infrastructure necessary to link the cargo area under construction on the south-west side of the airport with the Central Area. This included a 2,800ft tunnel between the cargo sheds and the stands in the Central Area where passenger aircraft were loading and unloading. To facilitate the speedy transit of cargo, the tunnel and its approach roads

Seaboard World CL-44 freighter
N228SW during its lease to
BOAC. (Frank Hudson)

were to be included within the customs bonded area. The contract was valued at £2.4 million, with the work scheduled for completion by the end of 1968. In 1966 Heathrow was the third busiest port in Britain in terms of value of goods handled. Over £500 million-worth was handled, this figure being exceeded only by the Port of London and the Liverpool docks. Construction work on the first stage of the £23 million, 160-acre cargo terminal commenced on 3 October 1967, with a target date for completion set at 14 December 1968. The British Airports Authority was responsible for overseeing the construction of the aprons, taxiways, cargo agents' premises, operations building and the tunnel, while the airlines were responsible for the building of the transit sheds, which they were to occupy as tenants on fifty-year leases. The tunnel was officially opened on 9 December 1968, and the buildings for the overseas airlines were ready apart from the fittings by the end of the year. The joint BEA/BOAC warehouse, with its stands for thirty aircraft, was lagging behind, however, and was not eventually handed over until 9 December 1969. The original plans for the area envisaged all the airlines apart from BEA and BOAC sharing a single communal import warehouse, but the airlines, which included Lufthansa, Air France, KLM, Seaboard World Airlines, Pan-American Airways, Trans World Airlines, Air India and El Al, held out for individual facilities and got their way. The new cargo terminal was officially opened by HRH the Duke of Edinburgh on 22 May 1970.

REFERENCES

BOOKS

Heathrow – 2000 Years of History, Philip Sherwood, Sutton Publishing Ltd, 1999

Time Flies – Heathrow at 60, Alan Gallop, Sutton Publishing Ltd, 2005

British Independent Airlines Since 1946, A.C. Merton Jones, LAAC International & Merseyside Aviation Society, 1976

The Complete Guide to London Airport, Sir Miles Thomas. Pitkin Pictorials Ltd

BOAC London Airport, BOAC

Gateway To The World, Maurice Housego, Thames Valley Art Productions

London Airport, Ministry of Civil Aviation, 1948

London's Airports, Maurice Allward, Ian Allan Ltd

ABC London Airport (2nd Edition), Maurice Allward and Roy McLeavy, Ian Allan Ltd, 1958

The Annals of British and Commonwealth Air Transport, John Stroud, Putnam, 1962

Bradshaws International Air Guide (15 Feb.–14 Mar. 1952 edition)

Heathrow ATC – The First 50 Years, Brian Piket & Pete Bish, 2005

ARTICLES

'There's an Anson heading straight for us', Keith Hayward, Chiltern Airwords – Dec. 1997

'From Humble Beginnings', A.C. Merton Jones, *Propliner* magazine

'It's An Ill Wind'. Via Keith Hayward, *British Airways Terminal One* magazine

'Speedbird Service', Brian Sullivan, *Aeroplane Monthly*, 1995

'BOAC Newsletter' (March 1947), British Airways archives

Various news items and articles from *Flight* magazine

WEBSITES

http://aviation-safety.net

www.airliners.net

www.air-britain.com

INDEX